HEART OF TOBA

HEART OF TOBA

BATAK LIFE BESIDE THE
WORLD'S LARGEST CALDERA LAKE

Nigel Foster

NIGEL
KAYAKS

Library of Congress Control Number: 2021900057
ISBN: 978-1-7364203-0-0 (paperback)
ASIN: B08SWLBFZ9 (Kindle)

Design by Nigel Foster.
Cover photographs by Kristin Nelson.
Maps by Nigel Foster.

Printed by Amazon.

Publisher Nigel Kayaks LLC
www.nigelkayaks.com

To my mother Elizabeth Foster,
always a great inspiration to me.

Table of Contents

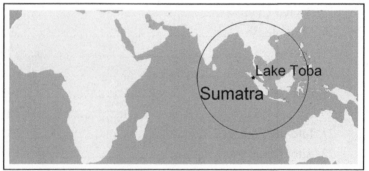

Map 1. Location of Lake Toba in North Sumatra

Map 2. Lake Toba and Samosir Island

1. Dance

As the music started, the *datu*, shaman, his ornately carved staff held upright in both hands, began to sway. His slender body moved cobra-like to the music. He faced the women who stood in line one behind the other, each bobbing gently, bending at the knees. Straight-backed and with expressionless faces, all rhythmically dipped and rose in perfectly imperfect time.

The datu turned, stepping sideways and back, caressing his staff. Stroking the dark hair affixed to its head. He appeared to love it, to honor it, to respect it, his head moving so that his trance-like forward gaze could scan down the length of its carved surface, and back again.

Now he swept the tip across the ground in front of him, backward and forward and around, as if casting a spell, or scanning for buried metal. I was minded of a dowser. Then he stepped forward. As he edged slowly and deliberately further, the women continued to bob, rhythmically, until, after a short delay they moved ahead in unison.

After one short barefoot step, they bobbed slowly down and up. Another short step, another dip. The procession inched forward, the datu at the lead turning sometimes to face the women, his staff tip hovering above the ground to far left, to far right, sometimes facing ahead. His torso rotation and arm movements almost like those of a kayaker, he lightly gripped his staff as if it were a paddle.

The music played on as the procession tapped its way across the grass, toward the center of the clearing between the houses.

Leaning out toward and over the clearing, the houses seemed to peer down, their façades carved in intricate patterns and painted in red, white, and black.

I was seated on a stone bench, in full sun, my back to one of the buildings. The sun flustered me. I could feel the burn of its tropical heat sucking my sweat through the linen of my shirt, draining my energy.

Beside me on the bench sat my wife Kristin, and around us the rest of our group. We were watching a traditional Batak dance, but as I was to realize, this dance was a ceremony to honor us, and especially me.

Mr. Saut Hutauruk stepped forward, a colorful folded cloth hanging down from one shoulder. He held another bright cloth draped like a tray across his forearms. While taking many short steps toward us, he held it up, unfolding and lifting it, allowing it to spread. He displayed it over here, and over there. Red cloth with white panels, patterned in black. There was a glisten of sun reflecting on golden yellow thread. Bobbing, and taking short steps, he approached me, draping the cloth around my shoulders.

I felt a little embarrassed, being at center of attention, more at ease watching from the back row, but deeply honored.

2. Arrival

We landed in Sumatra at Silangit International Airport at Siborong-Borong, on a small jet from Jakarta. Disembarking down the metal steps, we walked across rain-wet asphalt to the tiny arrivals room to await our baggage. The airport is located south of Lake Toba, the large highland lake, with its substantial Samosir Island which we intended to circle 160km (100 miles) by kayak.

Before long, bags and suitcases thumped down, hand-thrown through the open hatchway onto a short conveyor belt that delivered them directly to a bench of steel rollers. The confined space offered little room for both people and baggage. In the immediate scramble and scuffle for those prime spots at the front, the crowd became several people deep.

The bags logjammed. Nobody at the front moved to clear any items not their own, while several at the back who could see their bags, struggled in vain to penetrate the wall of people blocking their way. Nobody stepped aside to forfeit their place, yet no more bags could be delivered until the blockage cleared. Impasse! I wormed my way out and backed away. I could wait.

Priyo Utomo masterminded the coming adventure. His friend Ade Satari flew here with his inflatable stand-up paddleboard. Videographer Tandon, who also went by the name Don Seco, traveled with his long-limbed Malaysian girlfriend the photographer Allysa Shim, or Ally. I came with the ceramic artist and kayaker Kristin Nelson, my wife.

Kristin and I already knew Priyo, having spent more than eight weeks on kayaking trips with him in Raja Ampat, West Papua, where he worked seasonally as a guide. Priyo, slight of build and with delicate hands, might at first glance be mistaken for a teenager. Yet, with his dark, shoulder-length hair neatly tied back in a ponytail, the shadow of a goatee on his chin, wearing wide wire-framed glasses, Priyo has the demeanor of a Javanese scholar.

Style conscious, he often wears a pair of smart trousers of an Indonesian outdoor brand in green or khaki, and a quality t-shirt. His fingers are ready to check the heft of any fabric that catches his eye, and he is quick to note someone's fashion sense. Around his neck, he habitually wears a bandana or scarf.

Kayaking was far from his mind when he met and married Swina Montororing, an avid whitewater kayaker. She coaxed him away from his books, into kayaking, until the successful conversion became somewhat of a role reversal. Nowadays he spends much of his year kayaking, while it is Swina who leads more of the city life in Bandung, Java, raising their children.

During our time together in Raja Ampat, Priyo had often expressed his thoughts about Lake Toba. At first it was in passing reference. Later, "You would love it there," he tempted. "The architecture is unique, and the culture is so special."

To Kristin, who as a student had spent a year in Sweden studying weaving, he explained how the Toba Batak culture of weaving has diminished. "They used to source all the ingredients for their dyes in the forest. Some of that knowledge is disappearing, but you can still see people weaving outside their houses in some of the villages."

Sowing more seeds of curiosity, another time he added, "You know, the Batak have a paddling culture on the lake." Little by little he drew us in. In quiet moments through the summer, I found myself at home in Seattle between trips reading Batak poetry, learning about Toba Batak architecture, and becoming absorbed by Sumatran geology.

While we knew Priyo reasonably well, Kristin and I had first met the others in Jakarta while waiting to board this flight. Tandon, calm, stocky with a square-face, curly black hair, and a self-confident smile, was an outdoor videographer. He made his living on assignment, filming such action as off-road vehicles operating in wild places, and producing videos. Having studied at Regent's Business School in London, England, he spoke English well, and with the familiar accent of my country of origin.

For all the toughness of the locations where he films, he comes across as a quiet man, almost shy, often positioning himself to the edge of a group, yet keenly aware of everything that is going on. He had met Ally on one of his assignments, and they had got together afterwards.

Ally, tall, slender, pretty and a little shy, with long ringlets of dark hair, was a photographer and journalist from Malaysia. When she smiled her high cheeks bulged, narrowing her eyes up, like blinds closing. She had a lingering smile that seemed always to be there or poised ready to be there.

Tandon and Ally came to film and photo document our trip, planning to produce a series of short documentaries to promote and educate about Lake Toba and Batak culture. We could expect to find ourselves under the lens, or at the end of a microphone, at any time.

Ade Satari, fit, solid, and clean shaven, wore his silver hair short and tidy. Like others with an active lifestyle, he secured his glasses on a tether around his neck. With an A-type personality, Ade was something of an outdoor sports fanatic. Pushing hard as a top paragliding competitor, he had been *put back together again*, not for the first time, after a serious crash. Prompted to consider his future, he realized that his luck might run out too soon if he continued as he had. Flying was not all he wanted to achieve in life.

Coming down to earth, he took to water, another of his loves, reapplying his energy full pelt to focus on sea kayaking. He wore a smart grey t-shirt with *Sea Kayak Indonesia* emblazoned across the front in red, the club he founded with Priyo.

For this trip, Ade figured, recovering from a shoulder injury, he might be better off on the inflatable standup paddle board, *SUP,* he brought with him. He would have the opportunity to kayak too, whenever someone rode on the escort boat. Goal oriented, he set himself a distance challenge for paddling standing up. He would keep track by GPS until he achieved his goal.

We were surprised to learn that Ade knew Seattle. He had lived for a time close to where Kristin and I now live, while he was a postgraduate studying civil engineering at the University of Washington. He had enjoyed windsurfing on the lakes there, winter skiing and dancing. Trying to find something like skiing back in Indonesia, he tried rollerblading, but Jakarta was not the best place for that. Then he found scuba diving and paragliding.

Into the turmoil of the baggage claim came Priyo's wife, Swina; casually elegant, round-faced, with long, thick, dark hair, and a quizzical smile. She had expressive eyes that she opened wide to stare off to one side, while her lips, never still, danced quirkily around her face. She was full of nervous energy and excited to be back with Priyo after months of separation, Priyo only now returning from his season in West Papua.

Swina had come to Lake Toba from their home on Java, arriving a few days early to get things ready, and impatient to meet us. Having heard so much about her from Priyo, we were excited to meet her too.

Outside, two cars waited for us with doors open. We stacked all our bags in, cramming our bodies into the remaining spaces where we could, the doors pinning us together in the sweaty heat until the air conditioning offered us clemency. I reached for my seat belt but could not retrieve it. It must have been trapped somewhere underneath when the seat was last folded. To access it, we must unload the baggage, and since we were already moving, I could do nothing about it now. Our car chased the other in convoy as if late for a wedding.

Traffic drives on the left in Indonesia. There was little of it on the narrow roads, which led between fields and occasional houses. If there were few cars, plenty of people walked along the sides, either fatalistic or oblivious to our reckless haste.

We slowed behind a green coach. Peering from my back seat, I winced every time the driver pulled out to scan the road ahead. We were blind to the curves in the road, each time jerking back at the last moment in the face of fast-approaching traffic. I tried shutting my eyes but that was futile.

Finally, the driver made a break for it, speeding past the coach. I could see the approaching car, the shrinking space, and knew he must brake. Clearly, he would have to tuck behind the coach again, but no, he sped on.

We would surely hit. I squirmed. We were almost past. The approaching car flashed its lights and sounded its horn. We jerked in toward the coach on my left, almost scraping it as we jammed ourselves right in front. The car swept past, its horn changing pitch as it shot between us and the ditch. Although the sound of the horn faded, it continued to blare. The driver, at first sounding his horn in warning, continued to vent his feelings until long after passing. With a jolt, I realized I had stopped breathing.

I felt relieved when we turned into a driveway and stopped, the engine stilled to ticking against the sudden silence. The driver leaped out, grinning, and ran around the car opening all the doors wide. I unfolded myself stiffly onto the gravel, into the sun. The armpits of my shirt were damp. I breathed in deeply: the air smelled refreshing with a faint scent of flowers. I was still alive. I was here in North Sumatra.

3. Piltik and Coffee

Piltik Coffee reads the sign. *Homestay, guest house, coffee shop, restaurant.* Vivacious Vera Hutauruk, the owner, welcomed us warmly, "Horas! Horas!" ushering us into the little shop and dismissing our bags with a wave. "Leave them there, come on in!" Vera, short and strong, with a short-styled mop of silvery hair, was winning us all with her energy, her happy smile and her welcome.

"*Horas* is a Batak welcome! A greeting!" She explained. "When you meet someone or when you pass, you shout it out. You cannot just say it, you shout. Like this." She squared her fists as if to fight, straightened her back and took a deep breath. "Horas! Horas! Horas!"

Piltik is a family story. Vera's husband, Edward Tigor Siahaan, is a famous photographer. His specialty, corporate portraits, was just one of his talents, for he is a superb landscape photographer also. Originally from the Toba area, here at Siborong-Borong, Tigor ran his business from his photographic studio in Jakarta. Recently he wanted to return to his home territory and give back to the community here. The Toba Batak, I was told, were strongly connected by family, and although they travel, remain strongly rooted to their homeland around the lake, and often return.

Tigor and Vera moved here into a house, not far from the airport, built by the 10th generation of her family more than two hundred years ago. Vera is 15th generation, and as I understand it, all Batak families trace their patrilineal line back to the same man, King Batak, considered the first to settle by Lake Toba. King Batak was not a king in the real sense but has been since honored with this title.

Tigor, since living here, grew curious about the traffic that used the small road past their house. He noticed numerous trucks. What did they carry, he wondered? Coffee: always coffee. Coffee is a locally grown small-volume farm crop. The farmers pick the coffee beans by hand as they ripen. No single farmer could fill a truck with beans. All the small harvests are instead gathered by *collectors* who visit the farms. Amalgamated, this coffee is sold on to multinational companies, to be shipped overseas. This gave Tigor a business idea, one that differed from the established system.

Coffee is not an indigenous species. It was first introduced into what is now Indonesia by the colonialist Dutch East India Company, *Vereenigde Oostindische Compagnie, or VOC*. Under VOC, coffee growing began at Batavia, on Java, as early as 1696. But nobody grew coffee in the Lake Toba area of Sumatra until 1888, long after the Dutch government took over administration of the colonies following the dissolution of the VOC.

From the early days, growing coffee for the colonialists caused hardship to the indigenous people. The Dutch supported the pre-existing village social hierarchy when seizing command. They reduced the power and control of the kings, the heads of the family groups, making their life more comfortable but making demands on them. The kings had to make sure their villagers did the work and paid the taxes demanded by the Dutch. To produce those taxes, in the form of the required crops of coffee beans and sugar, farmers sacrificed land they needed for growing staples, like rice. They were punished if they failed to produce enough coffee and sugar. Prohibited from moving away, those who tried to leave were brought back and punished. As a result of this system, tens of thousands of those with only small farms, and their families, starved to death in years of poor harvest.

By 1888, the Dutch East India Company commanded the area south of Lake Toba. In pushing north, they faced resistance from the Toba Batak. Here, King Sisingamangaraja XII and his forces fought against the takeover, in a conflict which lasted for 30 years, from 1877 until the Dutch killed him in 1907. With his death, any hope of freedom dwindled. The people surrendered to be administered as a colony. So, as coffee came in, autonomy drained away.

The life of a coffee growing farmer under Dutch colonial rule is described in the novel, *Max Havelaar: Or, the Coffee Auctions of the Dutch Trading Company*. The Dutch author Eduard Douwes Dekker, under his pen name Multatuli, previously worked for a coffee company in North Sumatra, and then Java. Distressed at the plight of the local people under Dutch domination, and the corruption rife in the system, he returned to Belgium where he wrote a novel based on his own bitter experiences.

When published, his book caused a big stir in Holland, where the general population knew nothing or little of what went on in the colonies. As a result of public pressure, conditions in Indonesia started to change. Education would eventually create the awareness and skills necessary for independence to come about. At the same time, Dutch peoples' attitudes toward the colonies in Africa shifted. A whole line of colonial dominoes toppled, as more countries sought and gained independence.

The prominent Batak writer and poet Sitor Situmorang, read *Max Havelaar* when he was fifteen, translating the poem, *Saijah and Adinda,* from it into Batak. He claimed it was responsible for his interest in literature. Dekker's book has been translated into at least thirty-four different languages, but at that time not into Batak.

The late Sitor experienced Indonesia's transition from colony to independence firsthand. I had already read translations of some of his poems, but I would learn more about him later from his son, Iman, as our journey unfolded.

Coffee nowadays is a cash crop on many small farms. Most Indonesian coffee comes from farms of less than one hectare (two-and-a half acres). The Lintong Nihuta area around Piltik produces 15,000 to 18,000 tons of arabica coffee beans per year. Presented differently, a whole year's bagged production from around here would not even completely fill a single 20-foot shipping container, but it would be enough to make about 2.5 million cups of coffee. Starbucks sells about four million coffee drinks per day.

Arabica coffee is the most sought after, and it grows well in the lower humidity of this high elevation, for Arabica coffee plants are susceptible to coffee leaf rust, a fungal disease that thrives in moist and wet conditions and high humidity. In the late 1800s, nearly all Sumatra's Arabica coffee plants in the lower elevations were killed by coffee leaf rust. They were replaced in 1900 by Robusta, which is largely resistant to leaf rust. But although Robusta is better suited than Arabica to the lowland areas where the humidity is higher, it yields a poorer grade of coffee which fetches lower prices. That puts a premium on the coffee from areas, such as around Lake Toba, where Arabica can be successfully grown.

Most Toba coffee is wet-hulled. That is, the beans are quick dried in their parchment hulls at higher humidity, rather than slowly dried at lower humidity, before the hulls are removed. The slower method is called dry hulling. The combination of the low iron content in the soils, plus the wet hulling, gives the coffee a special unique flavor in the cup.

So, coming back to Tigor's business idea, since he lived in such a top-quality coffee-growing area, what if he bought coffee beans and branded them locally? He could source premium beans from select growers, grade them, and roast them, while his son, studying marketing, could develop the Piltik brand. Tigor had his business plan, and in the meantime, he could continue to accept such photographic assignments as he wished.

Of course, selecting the right beans is another matter. Dealing directly with local producers who select and pick only the perfectly ripe beans is one way to ensure quality. Beans grown near fruit trees acquire, like honey, some of the fruity flavor. But beans from specific locations can only impart special flavors if they are kept apart and not randomly mixed. The quality of the bean and how it is dried is just the start. Beans must also be roasted, ground, and brewed, and the devil is in the detail. Both Tigor's coffees, and his photographs, profit from his attention, benefiting from the tweaks in contrast and brightness. Each is an art.

But what about Tigor's wife Vera? She has worked at high class hotels and knows how to manage accommodations and kitchens. It is easy to see how the homestay was born. This location, close enough to the airport, was an ideal starting place for tourists, including us, who came to explore Lake Toba.

Vera and Tigor built a row of chalet style rooms, each adequately furnished with a bed, a desk, some shelves, and with a bathroom. Simple, clean, and airy, these rooms were located just a few paces away across the grass from the shop, beside which spread an inviting patio area with tables. This patio, sheltered by a roof, was open on two sides and partially screened with shrubs and vines. A welcoming place to mingle, and to linger with Wi-Fi, this was also the restaurant dining area. The kitchens lay beyond, hidden behind a room in which Tigor prepared and roasted his coffee beans. I could see his coffee roaster through the window. I admired Tigor and Vera's vision in finding a viable combination and getting it going.

While Swina found our room keys, ushered us, and helped with our bags, Vera rallied her staff to prepare our coffee orders. Then she led us along a winding landscaped path, bordered with shrubs and bushes and herbs. Many of these, she pointed out as we passed, she harvested for ingredients in her cooking.

Vera had laid a table for us on the veranda behind their own house, spreading it with savory fried rice, spicy sauces, and meat for lunch. "Please eat!" she encouraged, as her assistant carefully carried our cups of coffee, one at a time. The coffee was rich, and prepared as a latte, very creamy.

"Yours is made with arabica beans, and with buffalo milk," Vera explained. "Buffalo milk is better than cow milk. Much creamier." I could see the pleasure in her face as she summoned to mind and savored the flavor.

4. Rice Fields

Swina had already explored the area around Piltik during the past few days and was eager to show us something of our surroundings. I followed her with Syahrul Alamsyah, a white-water kayaking cohort of Swina, and with Kristin, through a gateway at the back of the property. Steps led down to a concrete deck, a secluded platform with chairs and a table, and an outdoor grill.

Two scarecrows guarded the deck, facing us from the edge of a rice field. One carried a big basket under her arm. Beyond, terraced rice fields of intense green stepped up gradually from the homestay toward the northeast. The rice fields were dissected by ditches and mud banks, vertically cut walls of mud no wider than the length of a foot. A stream ran freely down a concrete drainage channel alongside the deck, the sound of laughing water drowning any sign of the restaurant. The air, bright with bird song despite the scarecrows, felt fresh.

Syahrul, tall and lean, wore his jet-black hair short back and sides above his tanned face. Smart casual in dark navy-blue long-sleeved t-shirt, and crisp new khaki shorts with a carabiner knife clipped to the belt loop, he sauntered to the low wall, relaxed, about to sit there with his cellphone. Swina had different plans.

"Come on," she urged. "Let's walk through the fields." Foolishly I assumed she had done this before or had grown up in this kind of landscape and knew the rules. We leaped easily over the drainage channel, landing on the far concrete wall. From there we took a broad bank out into the field. Gingerly, we stepped from this onto a narrow dividing wall between fields of different levels, each densely planted with stiff, tall, rice plants.

Following Swina in single file we wobbled our way along to the next junction and leaped another channel. It was wonderful to be surrounded by these small enclosures, each filled with water and each draining to the next through pipes, the water running and gurgling beneath our feet. The sky reflected from the water between the stiff rice plants.

The sun felt richly warm, not sweaty hot as in Jakarta. The elevation here, nearly 1,300 meters (4,250 feet) above sea level, made a noticeable difference. The air smelled fresh. But I felt unsteady on my feet. To either side was a drop into rice paddy and water. The narrow walls, cut to hold back water not to provide walking paths, narrowed to the width of an Indonesian's foot and swayed under my tread. Syahrul, steady despite flip flops, moved confidently and nimbly along these precarious barriers, while I stumbled, slipped, and faltered in my clogs.

We were out in the middle, as if floating on a lake far from shore, when someone called out from a path on the higher ground alongside the fields. Swina shouted a reply, and the calls rang out between them. I have no idea what the conversation was about, but Swina led us toward the man, leaping across narrow channels, and wading a wider one.

The man stood in relaxed silence watching us approach. His water buffalo, grey, rounded, and plump, stood behind him, switching its tail, and tearing at the growth beside the track with a long grey wrapping tongue. A ragged rope was looped through its nose and back behind its ears, a lead from it hanging loosely to the man's hand where he held the remainder of the line in coils. Syahrul stood and helped us scramble up the muddy bank to join him on the rough track.

I watched the buffalo extend its tongue again to grip and rip, hearing the gentle sound as the plants tore. The buffalo's fur showed subtle markings. It was paler in a ring around each big dark eye, like tan lines from wearing sunglasses.

The man with the buffalo wore a white Adidas cap. A broad and well-worn striped wool scarf in yellow, rust brown, black and white, hung around his shoulders over a colorfully banded smart t-shirt. He wore blue shorts and worn flipflops.

Swina, looking stylish in her black trouser suit, with her thick dark hair hanging loose, stood talking to him, possibly explaining what we were up to, while he stood motionless with his hand at his hip, a smile sleeping on his face while he listened. Maybe these were his rice fields.

We left him and followed the track to a rough un-graveled road, then followed that downhill to a bridge. There, two men were fully absorbed working on a broken-down motorcycle, taking it apart with a few tools spread on the saddle as they worked. We greeted them, then left them to it. We climbed the potholed hill between bushes either side, past a skinny palm that looked as dark and sickly as a snag. Syahrul pointed it out to me. He said it was a sugar palm. The rickety ladder at its side, he indicated, was so the sugar could be tapped. "You can either take fruit or the sap from the tree, but not both," he explained. "If you take the sap, you won't get any fruit."

"What is the sap used for?" I asked"

"For making a drink, *Tuak*. Sometimes they use coconut, sometimes sugar palm. It is fermented. Not strong like liquor, more like beer. It is not so alcoholic, usually." He paused to consider, and then added, "Maybe the coconut version is sometimes more alcoholic."

He explained how the sap, a sweet milky-white liquid, is tapped from a cut into the flower stalk. "That is why you either get sap or fruit, not both. When you take the sap, the fruit does not develop properly. Look, there is a container hung up there to collect the sap. You can try tuak if you want to. They will probably have it where we stay.

"There is a legend that tells of a princess who was to be married against her will. She ran away and prayed to the gods to be made into something useful. She was turned into the sugar palm tree. Just about everything about her is useful. Those long stringy bark fibers," I could see the grey-black fibers, "they are made into brushes and brooms and rope. For thatching too.

"The fruit isn't so good to eat. If you touch it, it hurts your skin, and it is poisonous unless you cook it and treat it in the right way. So maybe it is better to use the sap for tuak instead of letting the fruit grow. The leaves are used for making baskets, the leaf stalks for fences, and the timber for construction. Everything is useful."

The two men on the bridge had got the motorcycle working again. It approached, laboring up the hill with both on it. As we stood aside, they greeted us, "Horas!" and slowly meandered past, up the hill, weaving carefully around the potholes and boulders, leaving the air misted with grey exhaust fumes.

Darkness fell rapidly, so we turned back, keeping to the road, and hurrying. It was already completely dark by the time we reached the last stretch; along the same road we had taken coming from the airport. Headlights blinding me, I stumbled aside each time a car shot by at speed. I felt invisible and vulnerable balanced on the rough, overgrown verge as each vehicle sped past so close.

5. Meeting the Team

We were early for our evening meal, which offered us an opportunity to get to know the others. We met Saut Hutauruk, who had arrived while we were away. A distinguished man in his sixties, he was fashionably dressed in long trousers, and a pastel coral polo shirt, colors that look good on men in the tropics. Saut was a relative of Vera and the main sponsor of our trip. He lived in Jakarta, and in his college days at the Institut Teknologi Bandung shared a room with Priyo's father.

"He's my cousin!" Vera explained, her expressive voice sounding incredulous. "He just turned up out of the blue one day, arriving from Jakarta." She laughed out loud and shook her head tenderly at him. He returned her gaze bashfully.

Vera continued, "He said to me, Vera, I am your relative. I want to stay. He did stay, for a few days, and now he keeps on coming back." She laughed again, and this time her laughing smile remained.

"My wife died," Saut divulged with sadness. Maybe that had given him reason to reconnect with family. And just as the Batak family connects and embraces, Lake Toba also calls its wandering sons to return.

Here also was Saleh Alatas, barrel chested, a thick carpet of black buzzcut hair, above a big bright-toothed smile, and a generous dark stubble-shadow of beard and moustache. Saleh was a geologist who analyzed samples, identifying potential coal and petroleum-rich locations. He was also involved in youth training, specializing in, amongst other activities, kayaking.

And finally, at last, we met Tigor Siahaan, his fine dark hair slightly greying. He wore big dark-framed spectacles open wide across his full rounded cheeks, and a smile below. "I think my glasses make me look Japanese," he said with a laugh. He wore cargo shorts and a pale smart-casual jacket over a dark t-shirt. Along with the confidence of a successful man, he displayed a shyness that set his success modestly into the background. Some of the many books he published, and photographs were on display here. There were books of photographs, portraits of prominent Batak businessmen and women, and hanging on the wall, historic black and white prints. Tigor would join us for a few days with his professional camera, and his drone.

We chose a round table and sat for our meal, which tonight featured tender fish: locally farmed tilapia. Then, after the table was cleared, Tandon unrolled maps he had printed for us. They did not show the modern names everywhere, he explained apologetically, but the terrain was correct.

"You can write on them too, and the paper is waterproof," he added, rubbing his finger on its surface. "You might want to carry them with you on the kayaks."

We would be kayaking so we brought some of our own equipment with us. Priyo asked if I would explain a little about my signature paddle design, made by Point 65 Sweden. I divulged how I designed the blades around how I like to paddle. Each detail of the blade shape affects its function, I explained, pointing out each element and describing how it affected the overall performance. Even the shaft diameter is an important detail. Change a detail, and the performance changes.

My kayaking philosophy is to gain maximum effect from minimum effort, and I love to maneuver accurately. With that in mind, I seek full control of the paddle in the water. It should be an extension of my hand, responding to the subtle control of my fingertips.

Priyo asked me to explain his carbon-fiber Greenland paddle too, his choice of instrument, and one with different design criteria.

I finished with a brief overview of the design factors incorporated into my signature float-vest. I enjoy the design process, and I find it particularly satisfying to work on products that I can use every time I paddle.

Saut listened attentively. I suspect he thought of me as a kayaker, not an engineer. But like most people I am a little bit of many things. I tend to get pigeon-holed as a kayaker because much of my work relates to kayaking. But in my case, I do not just paddle. In addition to expeditions, instruction and guiding, I design kayaks and accessories, and have published numerous books and articles on kayaking technique, and on kayaking adventure.

Saut was about my age, and a successful businessman, with a quiet manner and a pleasing sense of humor. But I could not fully read him. He seemed a little shyer, or more insular than the others, with a certain sadness and inscrutability. But he did relax. He made us all laugh when he admitted, abruptly, how he suddenly realized he was staring at Kristin's shirt. "For rather a long time," he conceded. "I hope you didn't think me rude?"

In truth, he pointed out, he was watching a particularly large beetle landed on her t-shirt. "Just there," he pointed, drawing our attention to the armored creature, some five centimeters in length (two inches), ornamental like a brooch.

"That really was what I was looking at," he explained, hastily adding, "not that there is anything wrong with Kristin's chest." Everyone stared, and then laughed. The huge beetle seemed content to sit there, so Kristin let her living brooch stay, ignoring it until later, when she coaxed it onto a flower.

Priyo had an agenda. He explained his motivation behind the proposed trip and outlined his plan. He conceived it primarily as a cultural exploration, to be accomplished by means of a paddling circuit around Samosir Island, in a clockwise direction. The objective was to learn about Batak culture, and at the same time, and this he directed toward me, to find out as much as we could about the paddling culture of Lake Toba.

Our journey, under the patronage of National Geographic, Indonesia, would be described as the paddling expedition: *Lake of Kings 2020, Lake Toba-North Sumatra*. Focusing on Samosir Island, our trip was to explore *The Heart of Toba*.

Referring to the map, Priyo pointed out places and objectives along the route. The paddling was to be our means of transport from one place to the next, enabling us to meet people and explore in a way that would not be easy by land. We would see the area in the context of the lake, but there would be transport available to take us to significant places on land too.

Samosir Island, rising more than six hundred meters (2,000 feet) above the lake, is a land that once could boast two hundred kings. The kingdoms were small and often at war with one another, so few easy routes were established overland. People used the lake more than they do nowadays for local communications. When the Dutch gained control of the region, they opened roads, so people travel by road rather than by water. But historically the lake was the easy way.

"When we reach here," Saleh pointed to the south end of Samosir Island on the map, "we have been invited by the owner, Mr. Omri Samosir, to stay at Onanrunggu in the most special old house. It was the house of a King. It is not a guest house, or somewhere people can usually stay, but he has offered us a unique opportunity to sleep there overnight. He would like to make our trip memorable. Maybe in the future, if our visit goes well, he might make it available to others. It is quite an honor." Saleh, with Swina, had explored possible places to stay, ahead of our trip.

"It's an old traditional house," Ade reiterated. "It was built by the tenth generation of Samosir family, while Mr. Omri is the fifteenth generation. I have seen pictures. Perhaps it is haunted. Maybe I am a little nervous to stay there." He and Saleh looked at each other solemnly.

"Me too, a bit," admitted Saleh. "Especially inside, it looks old, and dark. And a bit spooky!"

I was excited. When Priyo first disclosed his plan to me, a year ago, we stood gazing out from the shade of palm trees on a sandy beach in West Papua. There, at our feet spread a lagoon of the deepest blue surrounded by coral reef. At that time, I had no idea where Lake Toba was, what Priyo's reference to Kings signified, or why he would be so excited to explore a lake. I realized then how much research I must do, if I were to commit to joining him, and if were to make the most of my opportunity. Before anything else, I must find Lake Toba on the map.

6. Toba Geology

Back in Seattle, what I first learned about Toba was that it is a big lake: some 96km long (60 miles) and 30km wide (18 miles). At five hundred meters deep (1,640 feet), it is deeper than Lake Superior. With Samosir Island rising from within, it appears like an elongated donut on the map of north Sumatra.

Expecting to discover plenty about the lake, with its fauna and flora and its people, I was surprised when most of the information I could find was not ecological, geographical, anthropological, or historical, but geological.

Toba is no ordinary lake. It is the water-filled caldera of a super-volcano, the site of one of a handful, of six, extra-large active volcanic sites known around the world.

From Seattle, on a clear day, I can often see four or five snowcapped peaks standing up above the Cascade mountain range. In a roughly north-south line, they haze into the distance in both directions. Another ten or more volcanoes lie along that same line. Looking south, past Mount Rainier, Mount St. Helens stands next, at more than 2,500 meters elevation (8,000 feet), and 165 kilometers away (one hundred miles).

As a measure by which to compare volcanoes, the 1980 eruption of Mount St Helens was the deadliest and most economically destructive volcanic event in U.S. history. Fifty-seven people died, and it is said to have ejected one cubic kilometer (0.24 cubic miles) of material. That is enough volume to fill almost thirty million twenty-foot shipping containers, *TEU*, twice the global container volume shipped each month.

The crater left by the eruption has a diameter of a little more than two kilometers (1.3 miles) with no crater lake. I have seen the flattened forest, and roadside ash piles taller than a house, cleared from roads fifty kilometers (30 miles) from the peak.

By comparison, the volcano known as *Crater Lake* in Oregon, USA, another of the volcanoes in the same Cascade mountain chain, is a classic, very deep, caldera lake with Wizard Island, a resurgent cone, rising from within. When that volcano last erupted, it left a basin about nine kilometers across (six miles) after 150 cubic kilometers (36 cubic miles) of material was ejected.

That is about the same amount of material as was expelled by Mount Tambora in Indonesia, during its eruption in 1815. Mount Tambora's single event, probably the largest in recorded history, altered the earth's climate for the following years. The explosion was heard 2,600km away (1,600 miles). Between 70,000 and 90,000 people died directly in the pyroclastic flows, choked by ash, or poisoned, or indirectly from related earthquakes and tsunamis.

The next year, 1816, is known as the year without summer. As the ash cloud in the atmosphere shadowed the earth, winters became exceptionally cold, and the summers much wetter than normal. Crops failed, causing the worst food crisis of the 19th century. 200,000 people died of famine in Europe alone. A cholera pandemic then followed, killing millions more worldwide.

New England, Atlantic Canada, and parts of western Europe were particularly hard hit by the climate change. In Europe during the summer of 1816, disturbed by the glowering conditions, Lord Byron wrote his poem, *Darkness*. It begins:

I had a dream, which was not all a dream...

With night almost indistinguishable from day, he wrote:

casual visitors by stories of savage cannibals and head-
ers.

But for all the geological studies, surprisingly little is told
the people who live there, and their rich culture. At one
the Toba Batak were pigeon-holed as brutal, to be avoided
ssible. Yet, they were probably, like me, a mix of a lot of
s, which in their case included a talent for telling gruesome
some true, that would deter unwelcome visitors.

ven nowadays Batak are often characterized as harsh and
ess by other Indonesians. Is this because, or why, many of
become successful lawyers and business owners? Of
esians, all Batak make up only 3.6 percent of the
ation, with Toba Batak speakers numbering an estimated
illion.

s a culture, Toba Batak marriage customs reinforced
ship within clans, and even their rules of war were
singly civilized. I had much to learn about the traditional
e layout, architecture, imagery, customs, and legends, land
d lake use. Having read the few books available to me, I
l forward to learning more by meeting people, and from
n observations.

s Priyo explained, finding out about the Toba Batak was
our agenda. For my part, I had an additional personal
t in learning what I could about the paddling culture on
e. Yet I had discovered few snippets of information so far:
a foundation. In the past, the dugout canoe, *solu*, was used
hing, carrying only one or two fishermen. Longer *solu*
were big canoes, used as war canoes, and for freight.
d that, all I knew was that, like the native dugouts from
gton State where I live, these canoes were powered by
bladed paddles.

Morn came and went—and came, and brou
And men forgot their passions in the dread
Of this their desolation; and all hearts
Were chill'd into a selfish prayer for light..

If Tambora wreaked such devastation on the
sobering to realize how insignificant it w
Yellowstone. When this super-volcano in
erupted 640,000 years ago, it ejected 1,000 cu
material (240 cubic miles), more than six times

Yet when Toba blew up some 74,000 yea
even Yellowstone, ejecting 2,800 cubic kilon
(670 cubic miles). Ash buried areas of cer
5,000km away (3,000 miles), up to six meters
It was the equivalent of more than 18 Mount 1
Mount St Helens erupting together in one pla

When I look toward the distant Moun
Seattle, imagining two mountains where
visualizing ten of them, fifty, even a hundr
explosion equivalent to 2,800 of them bl
seems incomprehensible. It is the hole left, af
that magnitude, which holds Lake Toba.

74,000 years ago, when the world pop
was in its infancy, large enough numbers of
us to be here now. The event may not have b
genetic bottleneck that is known to have o
time, but it must have severely reduced the

Toba is such a significant volcanic site
that volcanologists from all over the world s
Toba did not even appear on the map u
linguist H. N. van der Tuuk became the firs
lake. Even after that, it was hidden in m

7. Museum at Baligé

It was misty and mysterious out over the rice fields until the sun hit, turning the fields rapidly from grey-blue to golden green. The magic was short-lived. The warmth of color drained as the light intensified. The moisture burned off quickly to the sound of frogs croaking, cicadas and bird song crisp in the air. At just 260 kilometers (160 miles) north of the equator the sun rises swiftly, and at the end of a roughly 12-hour day it sets just as rapidly, all year round.

Following coffee and breakfast we drove to the outskirts of Baligé, a market town at the south end of Lake Toba. Our destination was the museum, which was in and around a new modern building with generous windows for light.

The TB Silalahi Museum was set up by and named after the retired Batak Lt. General TB Silalahi, who played an important role in North Sumatran and Indonesian history. His personal part of the museum is devoted to the recent military, housed in its own building. Displayed just outside are a helicopter, a tank, artillery guns, and statues.

We bypassed both this section and the modern building nearby which is devoted to less recent Toba Batak culture and history. The latter we would see later. Our first goal was to see an outdoor collection of traditional buildings.

We were met on our way there by Eka from the museum, accompanied by other women in traditional dress. Each wore a woven ulos in red, black, white, and golden yellow, wrapped around the waist and hanging as a skirt. Two long narrow woven lengths were draped, one over each shoulder, crossing at the waist both in front and behind to also reach just below the knee. These were bound around at the waist with a long white scarf. Around the head, low across the forehead, each sported a woven band in white, red, and black.

Each of these Batak women had facial features in common; high cheekbones and broad jaws, and wide smiles accentuated by red lipstick. They all had great posture.

They came with us into the reconstructed Toba Batak village, *huta*, the buildings having been taken apart and brought here from other locations. Each building had a history and was unique, although all were similar in design. As in a real huta, the buildings were of different ages.

Traditionally a huta was established by clearing a patch of land and then building a single house, usually at the south side of the clearing. The house typically faced north. A granary, a similar but smaller building with a frame, roof, and main floor but no walls, was built opposite, facing across the clearing. Recognizable by its only six support pillars, the upper part of the granary, up in the roof, was for storing rice. The main floor would be used by women pounding rice with heavy posts. The women stood in a row to beat the grain, which was held in hemispherical hollows in a log. The clearing between the two buildings was used as a public space, for ceremonies, and for spreading rice to dry, while nearby land was cleared for rice fields.

The first house became the King's house, the first king being the founder and chief of that village. As his family grew, and the house became too crowded, new houses were built to either side. As needed, more grain stores would be built. In this way each village grew into a double row of buildings. Each building was

30

aligned facing north and south, along a courtyard or square that stretched east west.

Villages, for protection, would often be surrounded by a rampart, usually a stone embankment, mounded with earth and planted with heavy bamboo. The bamboo grew into an almost impenetrable thicket, making it difficult for intruders or animals to enter unseen. There would be two entrances, which could be closed, one at each end of the courtyard. While this defense might work against people, and large creatures such as tigers, there was still a danger from snakes, including cobras, which often hide in bamboo thickets.

The houses are both wonderfully artistic and practical at the same time, and many of them are more than two hundred years old. They have a distinctive style, with a curving saddleback roofline that dips between the high points at the front and back, and slopes steeply down either side. The front and rear façades slope outward, considerably overhanging the base of the building, shading the area in front of the entrance from the overhead tropical sun.

At ground level is a framework of stout timbers creating an enclosure for animals, or for weaving in the shade, or occasionally in the past for holding prisoners. The timbers are morticed together to create a stable structure, with the vertical timbers standing on boulders above the ground to prevent rotting. Longer vertical timbers constitute the corner frame of the main floor and support the thatched roof, its frame lashed into place. No nails were used in house construction.

The buildings are structurally very sturdy. Four huge slabs of wood stand on edge to ring the house above the supporting frame, the planks being tusk tenoned together at the corners. These massive planks are shaped like the side profile of a boat, upswept at the ends.

Steps or a ladder access the main floor from the front via either a trapdoor in the floor, or a tiny doorway in the low wall. A person climbing the ladder is forced by the shape of the entrance to bow down as they enter: a security advantage that makes the house easier to defend. Would-be attackers were forced to enter one at a time, headfirst, with heads bowed.

The wooden façade of each house is decorated by carving and sometimes also painting. By sloping outward, it not only shades the ground in front of the house, but also keeps rain away from the air vents, which are in the form of loosely fitted planks, and by the division of the façade into several wooden curtains, which allow air to flow up and in, or down and out.

There is usually a balcony between these split walls on which musicians can play, facing out, but there is also a balcony on the inside used for storage. This upper level is accessed from inside the building by ladder.

Syahrul pointed out to me that the ladders outside had an odd number of steps. I looked along the line of buildings, quickly counting, and saw that was true. Here there were either five or seven.

He told me how the builders often sacrificed slaves when constructing a new house. Before each corner post was placed, a captive, or a slave was decapitated, and the head buried under the corner post. Slaves were typically captives from feuding villages. Usually, they were well looked after, unless someone needed their head.

An enemy's head was buried at the foot of the entrance ladder or stairway, symbolically becoming the first step. Counting to the top, the total number would then be even. Everyone entering the building would insult that person, by stepping on his head both on the way up and upon leaving.

Inside each building is a single room. It is dark and cool,
 minated in daytime only by a few small unglazed windows
 through the low outward sloping walls of the east and west
 s. The windows can be closed with wooden shutters.
 We were busy exploring in and around the buildings, taking
 e details, when Swina called us together to regroup outside
 illage walls. There we lined up, one pair behind the next, in
 umn. Dancers, dressed in traditional regalia, lined up in a
 ar column facing us from within the compound. Music
 d, a wailing flute-like melody, with drumbeats. The
 rs beckoned. Stepping backward and bobbing in time to
 usic, they ceremonially welcomed us into the compound,
 we were invited to sit, or stand, in front of the main
 . Meanwhile the dancers lined up at the far end of the
 ard.
 was then, during the dances and ceremonies, that I was
 ed with the ulos, in red, black, white, and gold, which was
 around my shoulders by Saut Hutauruk. In turn, each of
 rs was also honored, presented with an ulos, folded
 ise and draped across one shoulder. It was a great
 to be so welcomed.
 wing the ceremonies, we drove to lunch at what I was
 a typical *nasi padang* restaurant. Girls dressed in long
 red red dresses greeted us and welcomed us inside.
 me, this style of dining, which originated from
 bau in West Sumatra, is noted for its serving method.
 e were seating ourselves a long table, dishes of food
 ght in and lined up in front of us in two long rows. The
 tinued to arrive, even when there appeared to be no
 left. These extra dishes were balanced along the
 third row on top of the others. With pots of soup and
 getables, containers of rice, various meats and offal,

A powder, known as *pupuk*, was prepared f
kidnapped from a nearby village and raised as part
until the age of 10 or 12 years. The child was ther
neck, made to agree to serve the family, and 1
pouring molten tin or lead into the mouth. This s
ensuring that the soul could not escape to retract

The body was then dried, while the escaping
captured and saved as the body decomposed.
were carved from buffalo horn, or bamboo, t
and the powdered dried body for future use. Pt
over the datu's staff, and small portions were l
holes bored in the staff, to infuse it with speci
staff was something to be revered, its power

The designs carved on the façade of th
usually decorated in red, black, and white
decorative motif, whether carved, painted
gorga. When painted, as here, lime was us
white paint, charcoal in the black, but l
enemy was mixed into the red. That be
house façade signified the demise of
reputation and status of the king.

The colors used in traditional arts, r
the woven ulos, had significance in
White represented the upper realm, re
living, and black the lower realm, or

Common decorative motifs, use
include the Singa, a monster lion-h
a long trunk-like tongue. A singa he
head, is frequently positioned on
Lower down, the fertility symbol
double pairs of female breasts,
almost always present.

ill
cu
sid

in t
the
a co
simi
start
danc
the m
where
house
courty
It
presen
draped
the oth
lengthw
privileg
Foll
told was
embroid
New to
Minangk
Even as v
were brou
dishes co
more roon
center in a
bowls of v

and different fishes, sauces and sambals, the whole table was heavily laden.

I wondered how much such a feast must cost. I was also dismayed at how much would be left over, wasted. However, I was reassured to learn that we would be charged for only those dishes that our group sampled. Any untouched dishes would be served up again later to other customers. Previous customers had already bypassed some of the dishes served to us. It was better to enjoy a whole dish, or to share a dish with a neighbor, than to sample a little of everything.

I could identify some food that lay before me such as dried fish, meat which was probably beef or chicken, and green peppers in chili sauce. But other ingredients were less easy to recognize. Dishes of animal parts such as tongue, lung, brain, and stomach and liver are traditionally served, but once processed, and disguised by colorful spicy sauces, it is difficult to identify the ingredients. It is not always obvious from the texture or flavor, so I was happy not to ask too many questions before sampling, for fear of being prejudiced.

When we stood to leave, the restaurant staff rushed up to ask if they could have their photos taken with us. Western faces are uncommon around here. It took some time, switching photographers and with a stream of devices, for each of the hostesses, servers, cooks, and cashiers to get their own pictures.

Our friend Harriet Huber had just arrived at Baligé from America, so we returned to greet her, where the museum would perform a second dance routine in her honor.

Harriet was, like Kristin and me, from Seattle. Harriet and Kristin first met each other at Kristin's ceramic workshop, *kRI kRI Studio*. Although it is a production studio, not a store, Kristin offers an annual end-of-year sale, clearing her studio of any surplus bowls, vases, and lamps, making room to start afresh in the new season. It was there that Harriet heard of Kristin's travel plans, to leave Seattle for two months to visit Raja Ampat and Sumatra, Indonesia. "We'll be taking some trips of two weeks at a time. Why don't you come?" Kristin persuaded.

Intrigued, Harriet said she would love to do something like that, but the trip in West Papua that Kristin described would involve more kayaking than she could manage right now. On the other hand, she was tempted to join us in Sumatra.

We met to explore possibilities before, wasting no time, Harriet booked her flights. Seeing where in North Sumatra she would be, she set aside extra time afterwards to visit an orangutan reserve, not far north from Lake Toba.

Harriet is a retired field biologist, no stranger to lone travel and unafraid to explore new places. But she started traveling before she even considered field work and before she was a biologist. She took off on a whim to visit a friend in Africa, who was researching elephants. There she met a National Geographic photographer, and traveled all over Kenya with him.

She returned to college, which led to her studying seabirds, and later came almost full circle back to watching elephants. Well, in this case not elephants per se: she spent about twelve years observing the behavior of elephant seals on a small remote island, fifty kilometers (thirty miles) off the Californian coast.

She later studied on the even more remote Pribilov Islands in the Bering Sea. And then, as if that were not isolated enough, she counted penguins at the opposite end of the globe as part of a survey in Antarctica.

You might think this agile outdoorswoman was born in the wilds, but she grew up as a city girl in Manhattan, New York, and majored in English. She pulls her shoulder-length silver hair back behind a colorful headband, and wears dangling earrings. Harriet has a cheerful disposition and an infectious laugh; her joyful outlook and outdoor propensity to take-it-as-it-comes are a tribute to her seventy plus years of childhood. I was happy to see her again.

Once everyone was introduced, we reentered the by-now familiar courtyard, *alaman,* between the houses at the museum, where we were treated to an amazing performance by the dancers carrying bowls. One dancer carried a tall narrow woven sack on her head, while each of the others carried a stack of several bowls balanced on their head.

Over the course of the dance, the lead bowl-dancer took a bowl from each of the others in turn, balancing that bowl in addition to her others, while continuing to dance. At the culmination, she still carried her first bowl balanced on her head, but also one on each shoulder, one on each elbow, and one on each hand. She danced with all seven while I held my breath.

Each of the other dancers took two more bowls from the stack on their own head, balancing one on each elbow, leaving just the final bowl on the head. Then, one at a time, each dancer stacked her own bowls, and then approached to retrieve a bowl from the lead dancer, carefully lifting that to the top of her own stack.

Throughout the dance, bobbing up and down, stepping carefully with their bare feet, the dancers kept their heads perfectly level to keep the bowls balanced. Everyone finished by dancing away in line, each with their original stack of bowls balanced on their head.

Tor-Tor Sipitu Grail, the dance of the seven bowls, is a dance that was exclusively performed at the inauguration of a king. It takes practice. Afterward, the lead dancer confided how, even after training a lot, she was so nervous she might drop a bowl. It took a lot of concentration and body control. Altogether it was a magical performance by the whole group, but especially by her in that dance.

The women said that the datu who led the dance was also their instructor, and that he was both a talented dancer, and a good teacher.

With the dance routines over, the dancers guided us around the indoor part of the museum. Stephanie guided Kristin and me, translating the signs and explaining what we saw. She was Batak, from the east side of Samosir Island, and spoke excellent English.

She explained about the wooden sorcerer's staffs on display, and the carved containers of buffalo horn or bamboo, with wooden stoppers, for storing the gruesome *pupuk*. Of special interest to Kristin was a section on weaving techniques, displaying the different traditional fabric patterns and regalia of the various Batak groups; Toba, Karo, Simalungun, Pakpak, Mandailing, and Angkola. Here, Stephanie pointed out, we were in the Toba Batak territory.

Cooking was over a fire, with three stones to support a pot. The fire was usually lit in the middle of the house, on a sand-filled tray to stop the fire spreading. In the display it looked as if the tray could be lifted, hung from the roof as with other suspended shelves that made use of the high space of the main room, however I was unclear about that. It may have been raised just enough to protect the floor underneath.

There was also jewelry on display, and knives. We could have easily spent a whole day studying the artifacts on show, but time was slipping away.

Outside, all the women who had danced and guided us around the museum gathered to talk with us. They offered such heartfelt warmth and welcome that I felt loath to leave. If Batak history is an important part of their lasting cultural legacy, so too it seems is empathy, and warmth of interaction.

On our return drive we detoured up onto a headland above Lake Toba, to a viewpoint that gave us our first real sense of the stunning scale and beauty of the caldera. The lake stretched away to the north and to the west, cradled by, as if in cupped hands, the rim of the caldera, from which the land fell steeply to the water. Across to the northwest stood Samosir Island, standing high above the water to block our view of the far end of the lake, eighty kilometers away (50 miles).

The skies were alive with turbulent grey bubbling clouds that churned and tumbled, letting shafts of sunlight fall between puffy cheeks. Splashes of brightness sparkled on the lake's otherwise matte surface, burnishing the cold grey into gleaming gold.

But as foreboding as the sky appeared in places, it was warm. To us, having spent the previous six weeks in West Papua in humid tropical heat, this air felt pleasant, cooler, and less humid. Below us, the elevation of the lake surface was at almost nine hundred meters (3,000 feet) above sea level.

A group of boys in their late teens sat near the steep drop-off with guitars, quietly singing, and drinking milky tuak. Girls posed for portraits and took selfies near the cliff edge. Around us stood sarcophagi, many twice my height: substantial edifices, some crisply painted and clean, others crumbling away into thickets of shrubs and creepers. The bones of the ancestors watched on or rested.

Back at Piltik, Vera ushered us all into the kitchen to show us how her staff would prepare tomorrow night's meal. It was to be a special meal, a treat for her daughter's birthday. Tomorrow we would eat carp. Several large-scaled goldfish lay on the counter, aside bowls of different ingredients which included lemon grass, water spinach, and colorful spices and sauces. Vera proudly presented her chef, who stood nervously in front of us all. He looked as if he would be more comfortable cooking than performing, but coaxed by Vera, he showed us how the meal for tomorrow night would be prepared.

He began by chopping all but one of the carp into big sections, including the head and the tail. Then he lined the bottom of a big wok with greenery, setting the first layer of carp on top of it. He turned to select some spices.

Silently and self-consciously, aware of our cameras zooming, clicking, and videoing, he spread each ingredient in turn, carefully adding layer over layer until the pot was full. Meanwhile Vera hovered, her excitement contagious. She eagerly introduced each ingredient, encouraging us to smell the unfamiliar spices.

"Here, taste this." She held out a bowl with what looked like small round seeds. I took one, and crunched it between my teeth, releasing a spicy, slightly acidic peppery aroma. As I rolled the flavor around, I realized my tongue was becoming numb, and my lips too. It reminded me of a spice Kristin's sister-in-law from China used, one that also created that numbing effect, but this tasted brighter. It was fresher.

"Sichuan pepper?" I asked.

"No, andaliman. Batak pepper. We grow it here," she waved vaguely toward the back of the room, "right here in our garden. And these?" She held out a palmful of cloves. Those dried flower buds were easy to recognize. They were probably the first spice I ever handled as a child, sticking them into oranges to make pomanders to keep clothes moths at bay.

Vera next brought out a stick of cinnamon, something I recognized by its reddish color and form, although I had not seen it before in such big hard rolls, about 60cm long and 3cm or more in diameter (two feet by an inch or more). Cinnamon trees are coppiced to cut the new shoots. The bark is removed, and the inner bark beaten loose and peeled off. It is this inner bark that curls into these quills as it dries. It had never occurred to me that such big hard sticks were harvested. I was to discover that I was mistaken once again. This was from a related species of tree: not cinnamon but cassia.

The next bowl she held up contained seeds that looked a little like chickpeas. Seeing my puzzled face, Vera enlightened me: "Kemiri. Candlenut." I was no more the wiser. "Don't eat it," she cautioned hastily as I took one. "They must be cooked first otherwise they are a bit poisonous." I dropped it back. "We use them to make a thick sauce, for rice and vegetables.

Once the chef had completed his task, we all withdrew to leave the kitchen staff to their cooking.

Later, at dinner, Vera introduced us to stinky beans. She was clearly amused as she explained them, cradling a large serving bowl containing the long green twisted pods each about 30 cm long (a foot). Each pod appeared shrink-wrapped over a row of bulging beans, each the size of a butter bean. She urged us to try them.

"They are stinky beans," she laughed again. "They taste stinky, but if you think they're stinky now, just wait till later!" She promised smelly flatulence, but Ade commented drily that the beans made your urine smell too.

The beans had a strong clinging flavor, in the style of raw garlic, raw cabbage, shitake mushrooms or horseradish, the pungency lingering in my mouth.

I nodded knowingly to Kristin. "Later," was all I needed to say. Everybody laughed.

Stinky beans are legumes, in the same family as all the other peas and beans, but these grow in bunches on a tree that grows thirty meters tall (a hundred feet), with flowers often pollinated by bats. The tree, *Parkia speciose*, was new to me. But I was reminded of the story of Jack and the beanstalk.

In the story, Jack is leading the family cow to market when he meets a stranger on the road. The stranger persuades him to exchange the cow for a handful of magic beans.

When he returns home to his mother, who was expecting a good reward from the sale of the precious cow, she throws the worthless beans from the window in disgust at Jack's stupidity.

But, in the morning, Jack wakes up to find the beans have sprouted into beanstalks so tall, they have climbed to the sky. He scrambles out of his window, onto the beanstalks, and sets off, climbing up into his adventure.

For me, that story was always both mysterious and nonsensical, but here I learned that some beans do grow into the sky, as substantial trees.

The tale itself is an ancient one, thought by some researchers to date back 4,500 to 6,500 years. It is thought possibly to have originated in the proto-Indo-European language. If so, might the story have come from a place where some beans do grow tall, such as India?

8. Baligé Market

Our launching site was to be at the market town of Baligé. Having lost ourselves in a rough and tumble bazaar at Sorong in West Papua just a few days before, with sellers heckling vociferously for business often under rough tarps, we were eager to experience this one. An area about the size of two city blocks had been restyled, using traditional shaped roofing in the front part to shelter the market stalls.

We entered from the street into a wide area with low booths packed with dried sea fishes of all kinds and sizes, including squid and cuttlefish. Beyond was crowded with stalls selling fruit and vegetables. I was struck by how calm it was, sellers watching patiently, not shouting for attention.

Farther behind were fresh fish, both live and dead. One large tank was packed tightly with golden carp, each almost a half-meter long (eighteen inches), thrashing gently in water aerated by an electric bubbler. But in other plastic tubs the fish were torpid, lying on their sides, seemingly lifeless until, following our gaze, the storekeeper stirred the water with a paddle, or a hand, stimulating them to swim feebly in the oxygen depleted water.

I felt sorry for them, struggling to live, for these goldfish were not for sale as decorative pets. They were kept alive in clean water only to keep them fresh for cooking and to clean out the so-called mud vein. The carp Vera's chef was preparing may have been alive when they were purchased. Tandon and Ally meanwhile crouched, cameras ready, aiming their lenses at sellers and their wares and occasionally catching us in the crossfire.

At the back of the market were tight cages with live chickens, and cockerels, probably fighting cocks, under domed wicker basket cages. A man sat on his heels with a blowtorch in one hand and the pale pink body of a dead plucked chicken in the other. When I first passed him, I thought he might be singeing away remains of feathers from the skin, but he continued to wash the blowtorch flame over the carcass for so long, I realized he must be cooking it.

Kristin was eager to find textiles, and we found a whole section of market devoted to them. Lengths of cloth of every color and hue hung above and to the sides of narrow corridors in a kaleidoscope of vibrant color. The intricate patterns, subtle colors, and the shadowing of the woven fabrics caught her weaver's eye.

"Indonesia is known for its ikats and batiks," she said, explaining her eagerness.

"Ikat? Batik? What is the difference?"

"With batik the pattern is created using a wax resist. The dye does not penetrate the wax. The cloth is dipped repeatedly, but after each dip into the dye bath, more portions of the pattern are waxed to save the color underneath. In that way some parts are not dyed, or only dyed once, while other parts may be dyed several times. The artist must plan each layer of pattern carefully in the right order for it to work.

"The dye often seeps into random cracks in the wax, which adds a characteristic crackle effect overall. The wax is finally removed. Look, this is batik." She spread the end of a length of hanging fabric to show me. The patterns were crisp, clear, and colorful, with random crazing where the wax had cracked.

"See here, the patterns bear no relationship to the weave because they are applied afterwards.

"Ikat is trickier," she continued, "The pattern is dyed onto the yarn before it is woven. When the pattern is in the warp, it is called *warp-faced ikat*. The yarn is coiled to the length of the loom. Instead of using wax, the yarn is usually tied before dying so the dye only reaches the unbound parts. The loom is then dressed by winding the tie-dyed warp onto it. Done accurately, the patterns should line up on the loom. You can check the pattern before you start weaving.

"If you dye the weft instead, the pattern appears gradually as you weave. That is more challenging. It takes a lot of attention to dye the yarn precisely and then adjust the alignment of the pattern as it emerges, one thread at a time as you weave. With the pattern in the weft, it is called *weft faced ikat*.

"Either way, it is tricky to line everything up, so ikat patterns usually look blurred. Here, look at this." She pointed to a cloth with a pattern that looked a little out of focus.

"Usually only the warp, or only the weft carries the pattern. When it is in both, it is much more complex to make. *Double ikat* is the most expensive because it takes so much skill."

As Kristin continued to peruse the textiles, Swina urged her not to spend her money on fabric yet.

"You should wait to see how the handwoven cloths are made in some of the smaller villages where you can talk to the weavers," she suggested. "I think you might find something more personal and unique. We can always come back here at the end of the trip if you want to, if you do not find something you like better. Come and look at the fruit."

Swina led us into the fresh produce area, a section packed with fruits, stacked neatly into colorful and sweetly aromatic towers. Here she pointed out those she thought might be alien to us, selecting samples for us to taste. The woman tending the first stall watched, nodding encouragingly to us as Swina held up a round purple fruit, about the size of a golf ball.

"Manggis or mangosteen," she explained. *Garcinia mangostana, L.* The flesh was white inside, tasting both a little sweet and sour. She passed a few to the seller who dropped them into a thin plastic bag. Now she fingered a yellow fruit the size of a small plum, round, or slightly elongated. This was dukuh, *Lansium parasiticum*, otherwise known as langsat.

The thick pale-yellow skin split easily, breaking open between my fingers to reveal white segments arranged like an orange, each in a thin transparent membrane. Swina twisted her face quizzically and tilted her head sideways. I tasted, and then nodded in approval. It was refreshingly good, both sweet and tart in a way reminiscent of grapefruit. This fruit comes from a tree in the mahogany family. Swina smiled and gathered a few of these to add to the manggis.

Some fruits here were familiar to me. Seattle stores sell dragon fruit and persimmons, and star fruit, also known as carambola, *Averrhoa carambola,* which slices into the decorative shape of its common name. Star fruit, with its tangy rhubarb-like acidity, often seen in fruit salads, contains both the toxin caramboxin and oxalic acid, dangerous to those with kidney ailments.

Swina paid for the fruit, and we wandered a little farther, stopping in front of a mound of red hairy or spiky fruit that looked like Christmas tree ornaments. Yes, my niece who grew up in China encouraged me to try these. I like them. The red, hairy, rubbery outer case of rambutan pops pleasingly to reveal a slick-surfaced, translucent, milky fruit with a vaguely visible dark central seed looking out like a blind eye. A relative of the lychee and with a similar flavor, the rambutan has the more exotic overcoat.

Swina selected a few, and we idled onward, purchasing a bag of the strange looking snake fruits, salak, *Salacca zalacca,* before pausing by a deep basketful of candlenuts, the slightly toxic nuts Vera showed us last night. I felt smug that I had found out more about them. They are harvested from a quick-growing tree of the same name, related to macadamia, and grown locally as a shade tree.

Threaded on a stem, candlenuts burn like a candle, hence the name. A single seed will burn for about fifteen minutes, so seeds can be used to measure time. The fat in them burns so well it can be rendered to make lamp oil.

Apparently, these seeds have been burned to provide light since ancient times. Some found at archaeological sites in Indonesia were harvested between 11,000 and 13,000 years ago. Redundant as a light source, candlenuts are now commonly cooked into a thick sauce, as Vera had explained.

I looked around me to realize there were just four of us together now, Swina, Kristin, Harriet, and me. The others had slipped away and were nowhere to be seen.

Passing now through a narrow gap between stalls, Swina stopped abruptly in front of a counter, behind which a woman tended a cauldron of fat or oil heated by a roaring gas burner. There was the smell of donuts. Swina jumped up and down excitedly. "Sit down! You must try these!"

"What are they?" Harriet asked, but missed her chance. Swina was already talking with the woman, placing her order.

"Two kinds," Swina explained when she joined us on the bench. "One is banana, dipped in batter and deep fried, and the other is made from cassava. That is also dipped in batter and fried but it has brown sugar inside. They are so good!"

As soon as they were cooked, we shared the hot round golden balls between us. Sweet and deliciously fatty, the paste clung to my teeth like glue.

We searched among the tiny stalls offering crafted and household goods for sponges to clean our kayaks. We did not find any, but Kristin drew my attention to bundles of graters made from flattened cans, upcycled, tacked onto wooden frames. The teeth were punched neatly through the metal, puncturing the painted graphics remaining from the original cans.

Baligé market was not always an indoor market. When the celebrated Italian traveler, Elio Modigliani, reached Lake Toba in 1890, he photographed the market at *Balighe in the territory of the Dutch rule*. It was then, and may still be now, the biggest market in the area. At that time, wares were laid out on the ground, in the open air. Containers of salt were carried here on foot from the coast, a one-way journey of more than 110km, (seventy miles), whether from Barus or Sibolga. Pottery and other goods at that time were mostly from the region south of Lake Toba, where the Dutch controlled production.

In Modigliani's black and white photos, stacks of broad-lipped earthenware pots can be seen displayed on the ground for sale. Women used these to carry fresh water from the lake for drinking, so they must have always been in demand. They were also needed for cooking, fermenting tuak, and for holding the dyes for dying yarn for textiles.

Modigliani describes the colorful swirl of men and women arriving, and notes that village chiefs, attending the market from areas not yet under colonial control, came in disguise, wearing common dress so as not to attract Dutch attention. Lines of women, frequently bare breasted and often with babies in slings on their backs, carried goods to and from market on their heads.

We regrouped at the edge of the market, close by to where a woman stood smoking beside a heap of durian fruit she was selling. There, a woman in a patterned blue, white, and black woven headdress sat cross-legged at the kerb, a durian fruit split open on the road in front of her. She pulled fingerfuls of glutinous, rancid-smelling flesh from the large spiky rind, relishing the dripping fruit, sucking the juice from her fingers. One by one she sucked the big seeds clean of the gelatinous pale fruit, setting them down on the road beside the rind. The smell was formidable.

Some consider durian such an obnoxiously smelly fruit, that it is banned from many hotels and public places. There is even a commonly displayed sign; white, with a red circle surrounding a black cartoon of a spiky durian fruit, with a red line across it. Just as hotels often charge guests extra if they smoke in a non-smoking room, many hotels will fine any guest who brings a durian fruit to their room. It would be futile to deny it if you had.

It could be the strong smell that makes durian one of the few fruits sought out by tigers in Sumatra. The thorny football-sized fruit can be heavy, sometimes up to 4kg (9lb). When falling from the tree, they can seriously injure or kill anyone underneath.

Writers have historically taken pleasure in describing its distinctive odor and flavor. Marsden, in his 1811 book *The History of Sumatra* describes:

> It is a rich fruit but strong and even offensive in taste
> as well as smell, to those who are not accustomed to
> it, and of a very heating quality... and... the rinds,
> thrown about in the bazaars, communicate their scent
> to the surrounding atmosphere.

Travel writer Richard Sterling is more forthright in Jon Winokur's book: *The Traveling Curmudgeon*. He described its odor as like:

...pig shit, turpentine, and onions garnished with a gym sock.

Alfred Russel Wallace more favorably writes:

A rich custard highly flavoured with almonds gives the best general idea of it, but there are occasional wafts of flavour that call to mind cream-cheese, onion-sauce, sherry-wine, and other incongruous dishes.

Anthony Burgess describes eating durian in *The Long Day Wanes, A Malayan Trilogy*, as:

Like eating raspberry blancmange in the lavatory.

One wonders, had he tried doing that? For that matter, had Anthony Bourdain, the American celebrity chef, prior knowledge when he described:

Your breath will smell as if you'd been French kissing your dead grandmother.

Nobody, it seems, can resist the opportunity to add their own ten cents worth or to catalog the comments of others, but I cannot think of another fruit that arouses such passion. For some it is a fruit to be tasted out of bravado, like eating the squishy worm from the bottom of a tequila bottle. For me, I compare its interesting pungency to the putrid smell of rotten shark meat in Iceland. There, Greenland shark is left to rot in the beach for six months, and then dug up and hung in chunks for a few more months to soften the strong rotting corpse smell. It is eaten raw.

The tricky part for me with rotten shark meat, in common with durian fruit, was getting it past my nose. But unlike rotten shark meat, often paired with a shot of Brennivín, Icelandic schnapps, for moral support, it is unwise to pair durian fruit with alcohol. The fruit can seriously impair the body's ability to metabolize alcohol.

Notwithstanding the love-it-or-hate-it reactions that even a single distant durian fruit can invoke, we would wait there beside these durians, in the heat, at that fetid meeting spot, until every one of our group found us. Only then, with our appetites stimulated by the wafting odor, would we go to lunch.

Meanwhile we were blocking the way. Squeezing to pass us were hand carts, pedestrians, motorcycles, and *tuk-tuks*. The latter were motorcycle sidecar combinations, boxed in to serve as a taxi, or motorized rickshaw. The driver sat on his motorcycle within the same framework that encompassed a little cabin, large enough for two or four at a squeeze. Nothing appeared substantial about these contraptions, the only protection being a lightweight metal frame with vinyl walls and canopy, and sometimes plexiglass windows. Some of the motorcycles appeared ancient, and most underpowered.

Vera had particularly recommended a restaurant near the market, renowned for its pork dishes. "You'll love it!" she had enthused. "You've never tasted meat so juicy. You must lunch there!"

We found the low-roofed narrow establishment, Rumah Makan Panca Rasa, at the side of a narrow street. We squeezed past tightly parked motorcycles and crowded tables in the outer dining area, finally reaching the innermost room. We were disappointed: the whole restaurant was full. Yet, since Vera had commended it so highly, we waited, jammed between the diners and the boiling pots. Flanked by grilling meat and hazed by steam and smoke, we dodged aside like matadors before the waiters as they rushed at us wielding sizzling dishes.

Finally, a table became available. We quickly cleared enough spaces for us all, stacking plates, seeking out spare chairs, wiping the vinyl tablecloth with paper napkins. The tableware comprised a choice of chopsticks, spoons, and forks, but no knives. Why no knives, I wondered? Both the spoon and fork are just an extension of the standard way of eating with the right hand. When you can eat everything using your hand, why would you need a knife? Besides, everyone carried a knife.

The dishes arrived promptly and scalding hot: succulent pork half-ribs with the tender meat falling off the bone, dishes with steamed vegetables, and a big pot of aromatic rice to go with it all. Positioning a bowl of rich meat broth beside each of our plates, the servers fully covered our table.

Pork is an anathema in most of Sumatra. It is only in this small Christian Batak part of North Sumatra that it is so popular, and in Bali, and West Papua. In West Papua pigs are sometimes booked as passengers on flights into the mountains. There, once the owners have purchased tickets, both passengers and pigs board together and are strapped into their seats for the flight.

Our serving of mouthwatering pork preceded several other differently prepared pork dishes, each one living up to Vera's glowing recommendation. If our dining continued like this throughout our trip, I would have to diet.

Within a walking distance of 0.75km (a half-mile) from the market was the Mutiara Baligé Hotel, behind which a narrow road followed the bank above the lake. From that roadside, we looked down at a tiny bamboo dock. Extending just half the length of a kayak from the base of the steep crumbling earthen bank, this was to be our launch place, conveniently close to the hotel where our provisions, sea kayaks, and equipment waited.

We strolled back to the hotel car park to unwrap the kayaks and line them up, side by side in the shade. They were good quality plastic sea kayaks. I was happy to see familiar kayak models by Point 65 Sweden, of which a blue *Whisky16* of my own design was set aside for me to paddle. We began to check the hatch lids, rudders, and foot braces but were interrupted. The cars were here to take us to our next scheduled visit, to the final resting place of the missionary Ludwig Ingwer Nommensen.

9. Nommensen

Fifteen kilometers (ten miles) roughly northeast along the coast from Baligé, at Sigumpar Dangsina, stands a memorial. It is locked inside an enclosure, surrounded by brick pillars that support a tall ornamental metal spear fence with an elaborate covered entranceway. This is the family graveyard and shrine of the missionary Ludwig Ingwer Nommensen.

The reason for visiting this grave site was yet unclear to me. Priyo was, in a way, revealing just the ends of threads to us, gradually introducing people and places of significance. It would not be until later in the trip that I could tease out enough of the thread, to see how Nommensen had worked himself deep into the fabric of Toba Batak culture. For now, since the graveyard gates were locked, we stood outside waiting for the caretaker.

Nommensen, a Danish born Protestant missionary, brought Lutheranism to the Toba Batak. On his mission from the Rhenish Missionary Society, he made the first translation of the New Testament into the Batak language.

By 1864, Nommensen was 30 years old and already living in Sumatra, when back in Europe the Prussian Danish war was fought. As an outcome of the war, Holstein and Southern Schleswig which included his island of birth, were annexed into Germany under Bismark. I do not know whether Nommensen considered himself Danish or German. Maybe he thought of himself as Batak.

A small man approached on a moped and stopped beside us. Impassive, he wheeled his mount to the covered gate and shut down the engine. He unlocked the entrance, without greeting us or signifying why he was there. We continued our conversations, alert to what was happening, hesitating to enter.

Inside, a tiled enclosure of black stone held a row of graves, each surrounded by a bed of loose white stones that were enclosed within a low, black-tiled wall. Nommensen's own grave, a neat white plinth surrounded by white stones, was topped with a sign beneath a cross. The other pristine graves belong to his dog, his two successive wives, and his adult daughter.

There too are the graves of his two young children who according to Pak Uli Lumbangaol, our driver, were killed because the local datu, *sorcerer,* considered them to be evil. Feared as *white eyes,* a native description of the Dutch with their blue eyes, they died, he said, their little skulls crushed like eggs with a stone.

If true, Nommensen persevered with his mission despite this atrocity, and several attempts on his own life. He survived one attempt to kill him when his dog ate the poisoned food and died. In gratitude, he memorialized his dog in his family graveyard.

Nommensen was not the first missionary to meet the Toba Batak. In 1824, two British missionaries, Nathaniel Ward and Richard Burton, searched for Lake Toba. It seems that the Batak tried to keep them from finding it. Failing to convert the locals, and never having seen the lake, the missionaries gave up and left. Unsuccessful maybe, but perhaps lucky.

More gruesome was the fate of two American missionaries, Samuel Munson, and Henry Lyman. The journal of their journey via Batavia, now Jakarta, offers insight into city life there, village life on the Nias Islands, and boat travel, in the 1830s. At that time North Sumatra was only partly under Dutch control.

The account also reveals their anxieties about venturing inland, especially since everyone they met advised against.

They left the Sumatran west coast town of Sibolga with a group of porters and helpers on July 23rd, 1834. According to the reports of survivors, who arrived back a week later, they made their way from village to village through difficult terrain from the coast toward Lake Toba. Before reaching the lake, they were killed and eaten by the Batak.

Nommensen was born the year they died. Following in their steps he must have worried, more than occasionally, about his own fate. But he established his first mission at Pearaja Tarutung midway between Sibolga and south Lake Toba after, by luck, avoiding a sacrificial death planned for him by a local tribe.

This region fell increasingly under colonial control, the Dutch making incursions farther north toward Lake Toba. Visiting Baligé, Nommensen concluded it was unsafe, yet he moved north to Sigumpar some years later, in 1885 or 1886, despite Dutch opposition and despite still considering it unsafe.

Later, when Toba Batak resisted the increasing takeover by the colonialists, and Nommensen felt endangered, he called on the Dutch for protection. He and his church were largely in support of colonialism. The subjugation of the people would make the job of religious conversion easier, and for their part, the Dutch would support any go-between who could facilitate their colonial mission.

In the corner of the graveyard was a little hut. The caretaker unlocked it for us to see inside. It was a shrine of sorts. A framed photograph of Nommensen was propped on top of a cube-shaped safe in the corner, a safe that has not been opened since his death. Besides that, the room held only a table, with an open visitors' book and pen, and a collection box.

Considering Nommensen died in 1918, this graveyard was very well maintained having been restored in 1996. Across the road from the graveyard was a fenced area around a school. Young children gathered there to watch us. Their animated little faces appeared fascinated by these three strange foreign adults. Each child was smartly turned out in school uniform, the girls in white shirts and red skirts, the boys in navy shorts. The boys' white short-sleeved collared shirts, navy school caps and ties, were gold-embroidered with the school emblem.

Back in the cars, winding our way home to Piltik, we spotted large sarcophagi everywhere, standing in places with a good view, or behind or beside houses. These multilayered constructions were often topped with a miniature traditional Batak house, with the saddleback ridge and outward sloping end walls.

These are reburial tombs, and the care of the tombs and the related ceremonies are still carried out in the old tradition. The bones of the ancestors are revered. It is customary to exhume the bones of the dead, and to reinter them.

Toba Batak typically only built a tomb for a man who established a new huta, or sometimes for a notable datu. The decision to build a tomb is based on three factors. First, the man must have grandsons, so that the patrilineal line continues, with many descendants. Second, the descendants must have economic prosperity. Finally, the man be held in high esteem. Tombs were not raised for those who committed suicide or died from Hansen's disease, *leprosy.*

The multitiered sarcophagi that are scattered across the Toba landscape usually consist of an odd number of tiers; three, five or seven. The top tier, the one often in the shape of a traditional house, is reserved for the man who established a new huta, together with his wife. The lower level is usually a communal chamber where the bones of descendants are kept on shelves, and where the coffins of the recent deceased are stored. The remains of descendants buried elsewhere are ceremonially exhumed and brought to the new tomb.

Before Dutch influence, only the most wealthy and influential could afford a tomb, as this was often in the form of a carved stone with a lid. The stone would be dragged, either from the mountainside or from the lakeside, to the village on bamboo rollers using rattan ropes.

This required the cooperation of many people, and could take weeks or months, during which time livestock would be killed daily to feed everyone involved. A traditional *gondang* band, comprising tuned melodic drums, deep rhythm drums, and wind instruments producing wailing melodies, would play to encourage those hauling. Carving the stone then required the service of a stonemason. Some stone coffins were displayed above ground, while others were buried under a mound, often with a banyan tree planted on top to prevent rival tribes from stealing the bones.

The customary procedure is still followed. The bones of descendants are still brought to the tomb of the village founder. The expense of a tomb and the associated rituals still cannot be met without the cooperation of the descendants, with contributions from either many descendants, or a few wealthy ones. All are expected to attend the ceremonies.

When the Dutch colonized the region, Toba Batak reburials continued, even though the German Protestant mission prohibited reburial rituals. It was the belief that a part of the spirit of a dead person continues to reside with the living, and continues to exert influence, which kept the ceremonies alive.

But there have been some changes. With roads opening from Simalungun and the highlands to the east in 1915, and later from

Medan, cement was brought in by road, offering easier tomb-building methods. Since then, there has been an increase in tomb-building. Many of the tombs we see are probably recent, although the ancestors they honor at the upper level may be from many generations back.

Speeding past villages, we passed buffalo being led along the side of the road, and lots of motorbikes, scooters and tuk-tuks. We were seeing Toba life from the road. I looked forward to tomorrow when we would see it from a different aspect: from the lake.

10. Sibandang Island

Our goal today, Priyo explained as we sat around him at the breakfast table at Piltik, was to kayak to Sibandang Island, also called Pardepur Island, some twenty kilometers from Baligé (twelve miles). There, he hoped, we should be able to see women still using their traditional looms to weave the ceremonial ulos. To reach Sibandang we would paddle west along the southern shore of the lake, and then cross a narrow strait to the island. We packed, preparing to leave most of our belongings behind at the homestay.

Before we left after breakfast, Tigor honored me with a photographic session in his home portrait studio, also with Kristin and Saut. He seemed to have a clear idea of what he was aiming for in terms of posture, props, and energy. I brought my paddle and float vest, and a mug of coffee. Before readying his giant camera on its tripod, Tigor turned up his stereo to shake the room with rock music, filling the spacious and mostly empty room with rich sound.

By the time we reached Baligé and piled out of the cars into a brisk onshore breeze, an eight-meter-long pontoon boat (25 feet) with twin outboard motors waited for us, jostling at the shore. It straddled the tiny bamboo jetty and bounced on the waves that rebounded from the steep bank. A small group of men and women, and children in school uniform, stood watching. They were probably passersby curious about the action.

Motorcyclists pulled up too, pausing to see what was going on. Having seen enough they revved grey fumes and snaked back up to speed along the lakeshore track.

We carried the kayaks and gear from the hotel, first loading the boat with those kayaks we would not need today. Both Tandon and Ally would film from the boat, and Harriet would join Saut and Tigor as a passenger to start.

There was no need for us to carry anything personally, for there was plenty of cargo room on the boat, but what little I needed for the week was so easily stowed in my kayak, I chose to bring it with me.

When the boat backed away from the shore to leave a space, we fed the kayaks one at a time down the bank to the water and lowered ourselves into them from the jetty. Then, slowly, we set off along the shore.

Battling a crosswind Swina, not having kayaked for several years and new to sea kayaks, experienced some difficulty steering. We paused while Priyo rigged up her rudder, and then with steering taken care of, she paddled ahead like a fiend.

There were a few fishermen out in small boats with canoe paddles. Eager to investigate more closely, I made a detour. Kristin and I greeted the nearest: "Horas!" He spoke no English and we spoke neither Toba Batak nor Bahasa Indonesia. Nevertheless, we switched paddles for a few minutes for me to try his. This was my first opportunity to learn anything directly about Toba paddling.

The bamboo shaft, at least eight centimeters (three inches) in diameter, felt big in my hand. The shaft was split near the end, so the neck of the wooden blade could be inserted. Then the bamboo had been neatly bound around with line to cinch tightly, securing the blade. The blade was nicely thin, tapering to a fine edge, and was broader at the tip than at the shoulder. It felt heavy to use and too long for me to easily wield canoe-style from the low sitting position in my kayak, but I liked how smoothly the blade worked in the water. Was the paddle designed like this, or had it broken and been repaired?

In the fisherman's boat stood a bucketful of speckled crayfish he had caught, their ornamental bodies variously green, brown, or grey blue. Their aquamarine claws were orange-jointed, and each upper pincer was decorated with a red flash. They crawled over one another, three-deep in the bucket. He lifted one out for us to see more clearly. It measured about fifteen centimeters long in the main body (six inches) not including the long thin feelers which extended at least the length of its body.

These colorful crustaceans, known as Australian red claw crayfish, *Cherax quadricarinatus,* are native to northern Australia and to Papua New Guinea, not to Sumatra. They must have been introduced into Lake Toba.

The second fisherman we met would not let me try his one-piece wooden paddle, which was fair enough. Yet he was happy to hold it up for me to see. The blade was smoothly shaped with thin edges, but long and narrow, only ten centimeters wide (four inches). The bulky T-shaped handle was crudely carved from the same piece of wood, not added. He, like the other fisherman, was emptying small crayfish pots. So far, he had collected only a few crayfish in his bucket. His boat, which resembled a transom canoe about five and a half meters long (eighteen feet) was made of plywood.

What at first sight I had taken to be litter drifting here and there around us, I now saw were fishing floats marking the position of nets and crayfish pots. Each was a repurposed empty plastic water bottle, simply tied around the neck with line.

Our support boat kept close so that Tandon could film us, and Ally could shoot still photos, but the sky was evenly spread with a layer of cloud, and the flat light was less than ideal for photography. So, after a while, tiring of the exhaust fumes and the constant noise of the engines, we agreed it would be better if the boat kept up radio contact from a distance, except in the most photogenic situations.

The coast was steep and wooded along the shore, with small houses here and there, but ahead, dwarfing any other structure in sight, was what looked like a huge wooden building encased in scaffolding. As we drew closer, I realized it was a partially built ship, about thirty-six meters long (120 feet).

The tall copper-colored timber hull spread gracefully upward and outward, maybe eight meters (25 feet) above the substantial wooden keel. Sheltering the top was a makeshift corrugated metal sheet roof.

This ship, including the keel, was shored up above the beach with props and posts, and all was encased in a hotchpotch scaffold, improvised from nailed-together logs, timbers, planks, and bamboo. It looked like a weathered crow's nest cradling a single giant misshapen egg, the ship.

Some of the vertical bamboo poles in the framework stood in water before the bow. Leaves were sprouting, reminding me that we were on fresh, not salt water.

I wondered, when the boat was finished, how it would be launched. It seemed impossible that the supporting frame could be safely removed from under it, to slide the huge hull forward, down the beach, onto the water. How would they do it?

Two men were using chainsaws on the beach, to cut huge square beams. They fashioned angled beams and planks in the same way. Although they worked mostly alongside the ship, in the shade of a lean-to shelter, the whole beach was rusty orange with sawdust and wood shavings. At the top of the beach, beside a small house with a metal roof, a hundred or more long planks of wood leaned on edge to dry against a horizontal spar. Ade called out a greeting "Horas!" and then landed from his SUP to speak with the men. We drifted and watched. Later Ade said he knew the person whose boat it will be.

It struck me that, since it is not possible to reach Lake Toba by navigable river, every large boat on the lake, and probably the smaller ones too, must have been built on the shore, like this one.

For lunch we stopped at a waterfront homestay, Pondok Berata Dapdap, where architecturally stylish new buildings; brick-and-wood chalets, were tucked into the steep shore amongst trees. Immediately behind, grassy slopes rose steeply 170 meters (550 feet) to the sky. It was still windy, but a breakwater parallel to the shore sheltered a tiny harbor, just large enough for our tethered kayaks to float securely. The pontoon boat, too deep in draught to cross the shallows to the little harbor and too wide to fit anyway, dropped the rest of our party at the shore, then pulled away into deeper water.

Canoe paddles hung from the wall of the veranda. Somewhere, there are canoes available for guests to use. The paddles, hanging by their T-handles, were shorter than the others I had seen today, each a good general-purpose shape with a broad squared tip. Each one was cut from a single piece of wood to the same pattern. On the wall near the paddles a plaque, dated July 2017, confirmed how recently the homestay had been constructed, with already several independent guest units finished.

Tigor, Saut, Tandon, Ally and Harriet, who had traveled on the boat, joined us at the tables, one of which was spread with white tablecloths. We ate a packed lunch of rice, eggs, and fish, each lunch wrapped in a banana leaf inside a paper wrapper.

There were hot spicy sambals of more than one type, to wake up our taste buds. These sauces are made primarily of ground chili pepper, with other ingredients such as shallot, garlic, and tomato, all ground up together. In Indonesia there are two to three hundred different varieties of this spicy condiment, some eaten raw, others cooked. Many, like one of those in my lunch, behave quite aggressively. With my mouth burning with chili, I reached for my freshly poured coffee with instant regret as it scorched my mouth.

After lunch, back on our journey, the wind swung around in our favor and we surfed along, creating big spaces between the paddlers. Swina made fast progress with Saleh, who in his yellow sea kayak was the more visible of the two. Ade on his paddle board was challenged in part by the waves, but more so by the direction of wind, which burdened his injured shoulder making it ache. Despite this he kept up a good speed. Priyo, often talking on the radio, lagged a little. Kristin and I chose to keep the middle ground, keeping both Priyo, and the others in sight.

Eventually Kristin, Priyo and I grouped together and everyone, including the boat, converged on the obvious landing place: a short fringe of shrubby beach beside a concrete dock on Sibandang Island.

This dock, supported by tubular steel piles, sheltered several small open wooden boats, all painted blue. Their resourceful owners had lifted them ashore there, perching them on boulders beneath the dock beyond the reach of waves and rain.

Schoolchildren clutching large books watched us, looking down from the stern of a small wooden passenger ferry moored alongside the dock. Adults sauntered onto the dock and stood gazing down. A row of slender lamp poles ran along the dock, each with the rectangle of a solar panel aimed to the sky. Below each panel was a white box, presumably containing a battery. It was pleasing to see the low-tech dock and boats beside simple but state of the art lighting, powered on-site by renewable energy.

Priyo stood on the beach talking into his radio. Eventually he turned to announce, regretfully, that we had landed in the wrong place.

"There should be another, a smaller dock a kilometer or two farther along the shore. Swina will stay on land. She'll go ahead on foot from here to find our accommodation, to make sure everything is in order."

That decided, our boat team of Saut, Tigor, Tandon, Ally, and Harriet, wandered back toward the escort boat, while the rest of us floated our kayaks again, rinsing our feet in the lake before folding them into our cockpits.

With Priyo towing Swina's empty kayak, we cruised wearily along the shore. The late afternoon sunshine reflected up into our eyes to dazzle, as we passed steep wooded slopes with palm trees silhouetted against the sky.

Reaching a short concrete jetty, we pulled ashore onto the narrow beach beside it. Our escort boat eased in alongside, and as soon as we had confirmation that this was the correct landing place, everyone disembarked.

Massive mango trees stood imposingly on either side of the path, darkening the way up from the narrow beach. Tigor strolled off the boat and up the shore, casually picking up an orange fruit from the ground where it had fallen from one of the dark-leaved trees. After a cursory inspection, he munched into it, both fruit and skin. He evidently relished its flavor.

"It's okay to just eat them without washing," he called down to us. "There's no pesticide spraying here, so it's fine to eat these with the skin. The skin is soft."

A local man standing nearby hurried up to him. He appeared to disagree. "No," he said. "These mangos are sprayed with pesticide."

"No," protested Tigor, "It is not allowed. I'm sure these are clean."

"Look," said the other, taking out his cell phone and flipping through images to find the one he wanted. "Look, here is this tree," he held out his phone for Tigor to see, "and look, it is being sprayed. I know! That was me there, doing the spraying."

Tigor's expression soured a little as he examined the smartphone screen. Then he looked down in dismay at the remains of the mango in his hand.

As the boat prepared to leave, taking Saut and Tigor back to the mainland, we shouldered our bags. Turning inland we made heavy work of the steep incline up a concrete road, narrow yet wide enough to drive a car. With us climbed a woman carrying a big basket of mangoes on her head. She walked easily, as if she were wearing just a hat, not a heavy load. I had heard that women, and men too, can carry up to 20 percent of their body weight with no more energy expenditure than if they were unburdened. But when climbing a hill like this?

Apparently, the necessary bone strength and neck musculature builds with regularly carrying weight on the head, starting from childhood. This might account for the generally good posture of the women around Lake Toba, and the balance skill demonstrated in the dance with the seven bowls. But it does not avert neck pain.

Head carrying is well suited for awkward terrain and narrow paths so, although still common around Lake Toba, it was even more widespread before roads were built in Dutch colonial times. If Modigliani's black and white photographs of Baligé market in 1890 are representative, a woman often carried a load on her head, plus a baby in a sling over her back.

When Hermann Norden had the opportunity to visit Sibandang in 1923, there was no road. He followed the narrow path that led to a huta:

I welcomed the chance to see one of the fortified kampongs, well concealed in the thicket, characteristic of the Bataks with their constant fear of an enemy.

The official had been there before, and so could find the hidden path through the jungle growth – a path so narrow that we walked in single file. We followed it long before we came to a clearing, where lay the walled kampong. Then we passed through a narrow, fortified, passage, which brought us to the open space surrounded by Batak huts, built high above the ground, with high pitched roofs. There was a scurry of natives and dogs and pigs and chickens...

I listened to the voices around me as we climbed. There was the murmur of Bahasa Indonesia, while behind I could hear Harriet's American accent, her conversation punctuated by intakes of breath as she tackled the hill.

At a bend, a narrow pigsty clung to the hillside, overlooking the lake. As we neared it, the bigger pigs stood up on their hind legs, with their front legs on the top of the wall, to watch us pass. Harriet was still deep in conversation, laboring uphill.

"Harriet?" Since I had stopped in her path, she paused. I gestured with my head, over her shoulder. She turned.

"Oh, my goodness," she gasped in surprise, "I didn't even see them! I just walked right past." The largest pink pig stood almost as tall as her, staring at her with evident curiosity, its mouth shaped into a smile, whatever its emotion.

Near the top of the hill, we turned aside to a paved courtyard in front of a row of houses. We would stay at a traditional house in the row, which had been modernized with the addition of concrete steps instead of a ladder to the door at the front. We kicked off our shoes and climbed up to see. Inside was one big empty communal space where we would sleep on mattresses on the floor.

Built onto the sides, and around the back of the original house, were newer extensions. There was a formal sitting room on one side at ground level, with heavy armchairs and couches in red-patterned upholstery, the tables draped in heavy woven cloth like the ulos we had seen. Behind was a room used for family gatherings, and for dining on a mat on the floor. Leading off from it, the grandmother's room, at least one other bedroom, a bathroom, and a kitchen. It was quite an extensive warren, and it appeared to be home to several generations of the family.

A rear staircase led down from the back of the original part of the house, the room in which we would sleep, into the eating area, which was otherwise accessible from the courtyard via the side room.

Having changed, and rinsed and hung our kayaking clothes, Kristin and I joined Priyo to explore. Kristin wanted to see if we could find a village with people weaving in the traditional way. Sibandang is not a huge island. It is about 8.5 square kilometers (3.3 square miles) in extent. Less than twelve kilometers (eight miles) to kayak around, it is at its closest point only a half kilometer (550 yards) from the mainland.

Sibandang Island is volcanic, having erupted from the lake as a part of the Pardepur lava domes some fifty-seven thousand years ago, about seventeen thousand years after the cataclysmic creation of the current caldera. Its volcanic soil is very fertile. Many of the two thousand people who live here grow mangoes for market in north Sumatra. Otherwise, they can easily grow anything they need for their own consumption.

We followed a road that contoured the hillside overlooking the lake. Maize grew in plots beside the road, tall and heavy with grain. There were cacao trees. Their elongated, ribbed, yellow fruits were blushed with red. Regiments of bananas bent upward in collars around the stems of huge-leaved plants. There were numerous mango trees.

Here too were coffee shrubs laden with beans. Priyo showed us how to peel the skin from a ripe coffee cherry, a red one, together with the thin flesh beneath it.

"You can eat the skin and fruit, but not the coffee bean itself," he explained. "That needs preparing and roasting first."

The fleshy skin tasted sweet. Inside were two little packets, nested together like halves of a pea, but in fact two seeds: coffee beans.

We passed under a decorative arch that reached across the road with a smart new sign reading: *Selamat Datang Di Desa Wisata Papande*. Welcome to the Ulos Tourism village of Papande. But we could see no village yet.

We kept on walking, occasionally passing a house or a small group of buildings huddled against the steep hill beside the road. Looking down between the trees we saw the comfortable shapes of old houses, standing like cattle, with the traditional saddleback rooflines and overhanging eaves. They were almost hidden in the shadows.

Here and there, yellow lights began to show as it grew dark. The light fading rapidly, we retraced our steps, more aware than before of the dogs, which barked from almost every building we passed. Chickens scuttled aside from under our feet. Motorbikes roared past, often with two or three people on them, and only some with headlights. Everyone gave hearty shouts of "Horas!"

Back at the homestay, numerous members of the family gathered in the room behind the old part of the house. Adults, teenagers, and children, all helped carry bowls of rice, chicken, fish, and sambal, empty bowls, forks, spoons, and cups. These they arranged in the middle of the mat on the floor along with bowls of water for washing fingers.

We all sat on the floor around the edges of the mat, to serve ourselves and to eat. Then replete, we stayed there listening and watching, but not understanding what was said.

Finally, when Priyo and Swina signaled it was getting late by creeping off to the privacy of a small bedroom adjacent, the rest of us climbed the steps to the communal room of the original house. There we prepared to sleep on the mattresses lined up in a row on the floor, with blankets to cover us.

I slept soundly but was awoken in the middle of the night by dogs in a frenzy of barking, just outside. Everybody else must have awoken too, for it seemed that for the rest of the night, each in turn got up and crept out for a pee.

11. Weavers

By seven o'clock next morning we were ready to leave. We planned to visit a weaver at Papande before she left for school to teach, and we would go by car. Syahrul and Pak Uli, had come by ferry to Sibandang Island to drive us.

We arranged to eat breakfast after we returned, but I really wanted a cup of coffee before we left. We found a filter coffee machine but no coffee. Then Tandon appeared with coffee to brew, but we could find no filters.

Not until one of the resident family finally appeared did everything come together: fresh water, coffee, filter, the required stack of items to raise the machine high enough to plug into the wall socket, and the correct programming. But by then it was already time to leave.

Tortured by having to leave the bubbling machine and the coffee aroma behind, we climbed the hill, past a tiny corner shop, to the narrow roadside parking strip opposite a school. There were our two waiting cars, but the doors were locked, and Pak Uli was nowhere to be seen.

Eventually, along he came, unhurried and relaxed, smiling widely. We squeezed into the cars and were about to leave when our hostess ran along the road after us carrying a pot of coffee and several glasses. We all burst out of the cars to thank her. We had our coffee after all.

We drove to the same village we tried to reach last night. It comprised both traditional houses, and some modern houses, with hard packed earth between the rows.

From the tiled porch of a low modern house of concrete construction, where we left our shoes, we were welcomed into the front room. There, a woman sat weaving an ulos on a backstrap loom.

It was the first time I had seen a loom like this. The weaver sat on a mat, on a low wooden platform, on the tiled floor. With her legs outstretched before her, and with both foot brace and back support, she sat just as if in a kayak. By straightening her legs, pushing back against the wooden back support, she could tension the warp on the frame. When she slid forward a little, the tension eased enough for her to lift a batten on edge, creating a tunnel between the warps for the shuttle.

Tensioning the warp again, she could tap the newly threaded weft tightly against the end of the fabric, then select the next frame to lift ready for the shuttle to return.

She worked deftly at the loom, until she ran out of weft. Then she got up and threaded more onto a frame, looping it around and around from end to end, occasionally through a gap in the middle between double center pins. She was winding it into a skein ready for the shuttle.

For this fabric, she wove with red and blue yarn onto red and blue warp, the blue dyed almost black in places. She dyed her own yarn, having bought commercial dyes. She showed us samples of the dry dye, in small jars. The darker colors, she explained, she created somehow using rice, but she was unable to fully explain. She screwed up her face, looking frustrated at being unable to summon the words in a foreign language.

I wondered if the starch bound the dye more strongly to the yarn, but that seemed unlikely. It was to be much later when I found a possible connection. I was reading the blog of the anthropologist Sandra Niessen. Niessen, an authority on Batak weaving, began studying it in 1979. She referred to a datu who explained to her how the blue-dyed yarn can be turned black by immersing it in the mud from a rice field. If that was the connection to rice that the weaver was trying to convey to me, it begged more questions; what is in the mud that reacts with the blue dye, and is that dependent on rice? Or does the mud simply darken the yarn independently of the color, making it immaterial whether a natural or commercial dye was used for the blue color?

In earlier times, weavers here dyed their yarn using natural ingredients from the forest. Indigo dye would have been used for blue, but that dye was not sourced from the indigo plant. Marsden writes in his book, *History of Sumatra*:

> *There is another kind of indigo, called in Sumatra tarum akar, which appears to be peculiar to that country, and was totally unknown to botanists to whom I showed the leaves upon my return to England in the beginning of the year 1780.*

This wild climbing vine, named after him, *Marsdenia tinctoria*, grows to about five meters (sixteen feet). It yields more dye and was easier to use than indigo plants.

Its elliptical leaves were boiled, and then soaked in the pot, at about 40°C (around 100°F) for twenty-four hours, to extract the blue dye. The leaves of a species of indigo plant, *Memecylin edule*, were also used, but these offer no dye. Instead, soaking the leaves produces an acid liquid, which when mixed with the dye from the Marsdenia leaves, acts as a mordant.

Yarn must be dyed multiple times, at least twenty times to produce a deep rich blue color. Repeated dyeing beyond this will eventually produce black.

Red, another important dye color used by Toba Batak, was obtained from the root bark of *Morinda citrifolia*, the Noni tree. The bark was crushed, and the dye squeezed out into water. A mordant for it was often made from the dead leaves of Symplocus trees, the leaves being high in aluminum salts.

Of course, nowadays, modern synthetic dyes are easier to obtain, require less preparation, and are more fade resistant.

The weaver, no longer at her loom, ushered us into an adjoining room where she kept ulos for sale. We all crowded around to see. There were some exceptionally fine ulos, tightly handwoven cloth in fine thread, and coarser but also beautiful fabrics. Everyone considered whether or what to buy, and we stepped outside laden with cloths.

As we stood there, an elderly lady approached. She looked dignified, standing straight-backed with perfect posture in her burgundy-coat with its embroidered front panels. Over it she wore a pink shawl, patterned in golden yellow and pale blue, wrapped around her shoulders, and knotted at her chest. A big bundle of jade green cloth was folded as a hat on her head. She carried a short, twisted stick about a half-meter long (eighteen inches), which she felt and rubbed with her hands as she stood, holding it like a wand as if she were about to cast a spell. Her face was heavily crevassed and sun-kissed, but her sparkling dark brown eyes and ready smile belied her age. This charming lady, the proud mother of the weaver, was in her eighties.

The weaver left for school. We, no longer in a hurry, strolled slowly back through the village, taking time to stand and admire the carved façades and examine how the houses had been constructed. This was our first visit to a living village, with old traditional buildings. Saleh pointed out how most now had a corrugated roof. "The roofs need replacing from time to time," he pointed out, "and metal is cheaper and easier to maintain than palm thatch. But the metal is noisy when it rains".

Pigs wandered calmly and confidently in the street, and chickens ran everywhere, some with broods. The chicks looked like yellow dust balls blown by the breeze, running, and tripping along behind the hens. Roosters with long gleaming green-black tails strutted on long sturdy yellow legs. There seemed to be so much going on that I did not know in which direction to look. Children played, and when I looked up at the adults chatting in the street, I was startled to recognize several of the women from the house where we stayed last night. One woman with a baby approached and asked to have their photo taken with us.

Meanwhile, ducks scurried past along the edge of the street, beaks probing under and between everything, in comical haste. I soon relaxed. There was activity around us, but apart from the ducks, there was no sense of urgency. All was calming.

Across the square stood a low cement block building that looked like a tiny café, but it might have been the front porch of a small house. A short bamboo screen surrounded this space. There was just room for the table around which a group of young men sat drinking from white coffee mugs, draping arms over the still-green bamboo barrier with cigarettes in hand, watching us while they talked. Above their heads, a brown bird hopped in a domed wicker cage.

I saw similar basket cages to this in the market at Baligé, empty, or with a cockerel inside, but not with a songbird. Most likely, from the size and color of this bird, it was a straw-headed bulbul, a prized songbird. Indonesia is one of the few places in its natural range where it has no legal protection.

The songbird trade, plus ongoing deforestation, threatens its future survival as a species in the wild. It is thought to have already disappeared completely from Java except for in cages, where it is bred in captivity, although collectors value more highly the song of a bird captured from the wild.

A three-day survey in Jakarta in 2015, checking just the three main bird markets, counted 19,000 songbirds for sale, of

296 species. There are 80 to 100 bird markets on Java. In December 2018, the Indonesian Agricultural Quarantine Agency confiscated 8,000 songbirds in ten days, in three separate incidents, all bound from Sumatra for Java. The capture of songbirds is accelerating on Sumatra, even as the numbers in the wild are dwindling.

I noticed more details around me as we strolled on. In the deep shade beneath the many mango trees, the air was heavy with the sweet aroma of fermenting fruit. There was coffee growing here and there. A concrete enclosure sheltered by the roof at the front of a building was filled with golden-orange heads of maize, drying. Rice had been spread out to dry on tarps stretched wide across the dirt street.

We passed a young woman at work, sitting at a backstrap loom in front of her house, while her mother, wearing a *Hello Kitty* t-shirt, stood barefoot by the door, smiling proudly.

Of the many old buildings on the way back to the cars, some appeared in better condition than others. It was an opportunity to look again at how they were constructed, all the pieces fitting together and locking so roughly yet perfectly to make these animated shapes, imperfection forming perfection.

Back at the homestay we ate breakfast outside, perched on the steps, or the wall, or standing in the shade. There were tasty cassava noodles today and eggs, this time in sauce. It is no surprise that eggs and chicken meat are staples here considering the ubiquity of chickens.

When Pak Uli and Syahrul left for the ferry with the cars, we too prepared to leave, carrying out bags down the steep and narrow concrete road. There we passed a man in the street, outside his house. He was pounding dried maize heads with a post, to separate the kernels from the cobs. He stopped to greet us, "Horas!"

"Horas!" we replied.

"Christian," he said, pointing at his own chest. "Christian."

"Kristin" replied Kristin, pointing at hers. He nodded knowingly. But we had misunderstood each other, for he pointed at me next and repeated, "Christian?"

After we left him and continued down the hill past the heavy pigs in the pigsty, he resumed pounding, a methodical drumbeat that carried as far as the beach.

Last night we secured our spray decks around the cockpits and bound the openings, to prevent animals or insects creeping inside our kayaks. This morning they sagged inward beneath puddles of water. I was surprised, as I was unaware of any rain in the night. I tipped my kayak on its side to let it drain away, and saw a large toad staring up at me from underneath. It was puffed up into a plump knobbly ball. Better there than inside my kayak I thought, as it crawled slowly away.

A crowd with a lot of kids watched the proceedings at the tiny dock. Our boat drew up, returning from wherever it spent the night. It looked incongruous here with its twin hulls, styled superstructure, and its white molded seats and table. Around its decks were stainless steel guardrails, yellow and green canopies, and banners. Our quiver of surplus red, yellow, and blue kayaks was stacked along its upper deck, blocking the top of a slide, which curved down and out over the stern beyond the outboard motors. The boat, with all its bold colors, looked like a children's playground, or a party boat.

Launching, we drifted in our kayaks downwind, waiting, relaxed and sun-lazy until finally all was ready for us to aim across the narrow gap toward the mainland shore.

***

In the channel we passed a canoe-like boat, with a man hauling a fine nylon net. He had a tiny inboard motor behind his seat, in addition to a canoe paddle. I wondered, were boats like this the last relics of the paddle culture of Toba? Would motorboats obviate the need to paddle? With the original canoe designs here constricted by the dimensions of a log, would future fishing boats become wider, and motors bigger?

Beyond, we saw what appeared to be two traditional houses, in a bay, and detoured to look more closely. There were the distinctive drooping rooflines, but from closer we could see that they were modern houses, with large, glazed windows on the ground floor. It was only the upper storey of each with the roof that looked like a traditional building. The upper part may have been original, with the lower level modernized. If not, maybe the upper storey was added in the architectural style of the older houses as a nod to tradition.

The houses stood looking out over the water from a small village with a church. People lined the shore there, fishing with rod and line. A dragon boat, decorated in red and white, was moored by the shore. Was dragon boat racing for sport the new direction that paddling was taking here, I wondered? We approached, but when I took out my camera, someone called out urgently to us.

Saleh translated, we were welcomed to photograph the boat, but please, not to photograph the fishing platform floating out in the bay. The structure was illegal; they could get into trouble.

Dragon boats have been raced in China for 2,000 years and were made of various kinds of timber, depending on the location. Teak was often used, and the boats were most likely dugouts to begin with. That makes them resemble in many ways the *solu bolon*, the long canoe once used on Lake Toba. Comparable in dimensions, they too are propelled by single-bladed paddles and I expect offer similar performance.

Rounding the next headland, we were met by the view of a deep bay, almost five kilometers long but only about 1.6km across at its neck (three miles long, one mile across the neck). The steep green scarp, sloping up more than three hundred meters (1,000 feet) all around it, made it appear almost like a second, miniature caldera, joined at its edge to the larger Toba caldera. Geologically it is simply part of the main structure. We had reached the entrance to the valley of Bakara, the village toward which we headed.

Finally, we heard the buzzing of a drone approaching. Looking in that direction we spotted Saut on the shore at the far end of the bay in front of a green building. Tigor stood with him, waving. We cruised the final distance to where Tigor now stood behind a camera with a long lens.

Priyo did not join us just there, choosing to land a little farther down the shore. Was that where we should go? Kristin thought so. I was undecided. Since Ade and Saleh had by now landed here, I joined them as soon as Tigor was satisfied with his photo session. We stacked our kayaks and the SUP neatly on the paved promenade in front of the new green building. Syahrul took our bags in his pickup, while we walked to our accommodation. We had reached the historically significant Bakara.

12. Bakara

"Your accommodation will be in that low house with the corrugated metal roof," Priyo pointed. Beside the house, a vegetable plot hid beneath a waist-high forest of bare sticks haphazardly laced with white string. A wall of fine black netting, also held up by sticks, surrounded the plot, both net and string a caution to now-hidden marauders. The house stood by a junction, on a street with a mixture of little traditional houses, and simpler more modern ones.

In front of each of the older houses, which were all built high above the ground on timber frames, a ladder climbed very steeply to tiny double doors just one meter tall (three feet) in the overhanging front wall. This low wall sloped out at 30 degrees from vertical. This house construction appeared the same as at the museum, but smaller and lacking any decorative carving or painting. In place of thatch, the roofs were clad in corrugated metal sheet, now rusted, which preserved the drooping saddleback ridge and overhanging eaves. Bakara was founded in the 1320s. I wondered how old these houses were.

The house where we would stay, set back from the white cement street by two meters, was elevated above the dusty verge to the height of three concrete steps. We left our shoes on the steps and entered a spacious living room. A few chairs stood against the white painted horizontal wall boards. Large colorful mats covered the floor. On a desk in one corner, below a shelf with books, a cloth covered a little computer screen. Curtains concealed storage at one end while behind bright orange curtains at the other, doorways led into small bedrooms. One of those rooms was our hosts' bedroom. Tandon and Ally requisitioned the other.

At the back of the living room, steps dropped into a kitchen with a cement floor at ground level, and open shelves. Within the kitchen, a low brick wall sectioned off the bathroom.

Priyo, Swina and Saleh left us to walk across the fields to where they would stay. Just four of us would sleep in the big room later, but our day still lay ahead.

Syahrul collected us in the pickup. The concrete road, which led between fields from beside the house to the part of the village where Priyo was staying, was barely wide enough for one vehicle. We drove slowly along it and into a tight gap between two buildings. We emerged into a part of the village with many more traditional houses, all with metal roofs and all looking weathered. But then, the newer structures looked equally worn. They bore a pleasing patina, rather than appearing dilapidated.

Having picked up Priyo and the others from one of the small old houses, where they would stay tonight, we continued until we reached a restaurant on the shore of Bakara Bay. There, beneath a blue-painted metal roof stretched a long open barn of a room. Tables ran the whole length, facing the breeze blowing in from the water. Paper napkins lifted and flew from the tables, and around the floor. Beside the restaurant was an open-air swimming pool with a long plastic slide, the pool empty of guests.

We were still eating; fish, with rice and sambal, when Iman Situmorang arrived. A strongly built, regal, man with a receding hairline, buzzcut salt and pepper hair, and thick dark eyebrows, Iman moved confidently from one to another through our group, his big hands greeting with a strong handshake as he introduced himself. Wearing blue jeans, and a jade button-down t-shirt under a thin purple jacket, he held a sturdy black glasses case from which he frequently produced a pair of wire-framed reading glasses, which he seemed undecided whether to use or not. His father, he explained, was Sitor Situmorang, the famous Batak writer, journalist, and poet.

I had read about Sitor Situmorang and how he lived through the period of change, when Indonesia gained independence from the Dutch after the Second Word War. He was born in 1923 at Harian Boho, a little farther north on Lake Toba, into a high-status Batak family. He studied at Sibolga, and then Jakarta, receiving a privileged Dutch-style education and studying mostly European literature and Dutch language. He later studied cinematography at the University of California in USA.

Beginning his career as a journalist at the end of the Second World War, Sitor subsequently spent three years in Paris and Amsterdam studying European culture. His writing, as a prominent member of the Institute of National Culture, tied him to Sukarno. Sukarno was the man who led the country to Independence after the Second World War, becoming the first president of Indonesia. After President Sukarno's fall from favor, Sitor was imprisoned for his writing. He was held without trial from 1967, until 1976, before being released without charge.

Sitor had six children with his first wife, Tio Minar Gultom, who died in 1996. The next year he married Barbara Brouwer and joined her in the Netherlands. Sitor died in December 2014 at his home there, aged ninety-one. According to his wishes, he was buried under a commemorative river rock at Harian Boho, his birthplace.

Sitor Situmorang is well known for his poetry which is often on the themes of travel, wanderlust, and love. But he also published collections of short stories and wrote non-fiction. He was seemingly torn between the urge to roam and explore, and a longing for home within the cradle of the Toba caldera.

One of his books of poems, translated into English by John H. McGlynn, is published under the title, *To Love, To Wander: The Poetry of Sitor Situmorang.* I read those poems before coming to Toba, on Priyo's recommendation. I later found two books of Sitor's short stories, *Red Gerberas* and *Oceans of Longing,* also available in English.

We were honored to have Iman join us for the next few days. He would help guide us, showing us some significant places of cultural and historical significance around this part of the lake. His depth of knowledge and understanding is formidable, and his command of English is remarkable.

A brief drive away, we parked the cars at the roadside and scrambled up a short track to see the sacred spring, Aek Sipangolu, *Life Giving Water.* In a narrow gully, a fast current of clear water ran between concrete walls. There we stopped at a tight corner in the pathway where, shaded by a roof, the air felt cool by the rushing water. Flies hovered around us in the shadow. Kristin seized the moment to cool her feet in the flow, prompting Swina to throw off her shoes too, dangling her legs into the caressing water.

This spring, Iman explained, is said to have originated when King Sisingamangaraja 1st was riding past on his white elephant. His elephant needed a drink, so the king prayed, and struck the rock with his wand. The stream that sprang up here has flowed ever since. The water is said to have healing properties, so downstream, below the road bridge, is a swimming pool where people can bathe and pray for a cure.

We returned toward Bakara, our next destination Istana Sisingamangaraja, the palace of the kings Sisingamangaraja, a little more than two kilometers inland (1.5 miles).

13. Sisingamangaraja's Palace

The palace sits on the lower slopes of the hillside, overlooking the flat valley floor. Located at the village, huta Lumban Raja, it was the seat of the Sisingamangaraja hereditary government from King Sisingamangaraja I, the one with the white elephant, until Sisingamangaraja XII, who died fighting against colonization by the Dutch. That is, from the mid-1500s until 1907.

Chatting amongst ourselves, we had just begun to climb the steps, toward an archway with information boards, when Iman Situmorang, ahead, stopped and turned. We gathered around to hear him explain how this commemorative site was constructed by the government to mimic the extent and grandeur of the palace at its original location.

The memorial beside the road, he pointed out, was dedicated to Si Raja Oloan, the founder of the village, huta Lumban Raja. Si Raja Oloan's second wife, Boru Pasaribu, gave birth to a son, who became the first of the twelve kings Sisingamangaraja.

The future king is said to have been born farther up the Bakara valley, in a cave, at a place called Tombak Sulusulu, or spear of Sulusulu. When he was grown, he traveled to Barus on the coast to find his uncle, King Uti, who tested him and verified that he was worthy to be King Sisingamangaraja. He returned with, amongst other symbols, the white elephant.

Distracting us from Iman, a woman at the side of the steps offered mangoes to anyone who would like one. Those close enough to where she sat, took, and ate the soft-skinned fruit, juice dripping from the ripe flesh. Iman paused, and then continued.

By the late 1800s the Dutch already controlled a wide area inland from Sibolga. However, their attempts to take over the region of Aceh, northernmost Sumatra, were repelled by the fierce fighting of the mostly Muslim Aceh people. Now they planned to extend their control northward into Batak territory and Lake Toba from their stronghold around Sibolga.

King Sisingamangaraja XII, who was born here in Bakara, gathered opposing forces, recruiting also from Aceh.

Seeing how the missionaries supported the advance of the Dutch, King Sisingamangaraja XII, according to Nommensen, sent an envoy to threaten the Christians. Nommensen requested protection from the Dutch, and the Dutch appear to have used the threats on Nommensen as an excuse to invade the surrounding area.

Countering the continued Toba resistance, and desperate to learn the whereabouts of King Sisingamangaraja XII, they began to burn villages and torture and kill captives. Nommensen accompanied the troops for four months in 1878 as an interpreter, advising which villages to raid and burn. During this time dozens of Batak villages were destroyed. The royal palace here in Bakara was burned to the ground.

Nommensen was ultimately rewarded by the Dutch for his assistance, with compensation of 1,000 guilders, a considerable sum in those days, and was granted the Dutch Order of Orange Nassua.

King Sisingamangaraja XII continued to fight, promising to carry on until the last drop of blood to expel the Dutch from the country. He was true to his cause for 30 years until, on June 17th, 1907, along with his 17-year-old daughter and two of his sons, he was shot and killed.

We made our way slowly to the top of the steps, where we took off our shoes in respect to stand facing the memorial to the Kings Sisingamangaraja I-XI.

Iman explained how King Sisingamangaraja XII was not buried here. His bones lie in state at Baligé as a National Hero. Also, only the head of King Sisingamangaraja X is buried here, for his body was buried at Butar where he was killed.

The bones of King Sisingamangaraja XI were taken by King Sisingamangaraja XII for safety when Bakara was under threat, to prevent them falling into the hands of the Dutch. They were first carried to Doluk Sanggul, a few kilometers inland to the southwest on higher ground, and later a little north to Huta Paung. When Indonesia gained independence, the bones were moved again, this time to Soposurung, Baligé.

The Sisingamangaraja family has since rebuilt the tomb at Bakara. The bones of King Sisingamangaraja XI were ceremonially returned in 1975 to the place he would have considered home, to rest in the family tomb having been away for 105 years.

To the side of the tomb stands the palace, four imposing buildings, side by side, ornately decorated in red, black, and white, including *Rumah Bolon*, the King's House. But these are not buildings that the Rajas Sisingamangaraja would have recognized. These are new. All the previous ones were burned down.

The first palace was burnt by Tuanko Rao's troops in 1825. Tuanko was an Islamic fanatic who by account, in what is known as the Padri War, burned villages, and killed indiscriminately from West Sumatra all the way north to Lake Toba.

He is said to have been responsible for the death of King Sisingamangaraja X, having tricked the King into meeting him in Butar under the pretense of reconciliation. There, it seems, either he or one of his men took out a concealed knife and cut off the unsuspecting King's head.

Tuanko Rao's troops withdrew from the Lake Toba area, back to western Sumatra, when a plague of cholera followed the massacres, striking down his troops. It is thought the disease spread when so many bodies were left unburied. After the slaughter of villagers, and the taking of slaves who were led south, there was nobody left to deal with the dead.

Turning now to fight against the Dutch, who were expanding their control of the territory, Tuanko Rao was eventually injured and captured by them in 1833. Sent to exile, he died soon after. Allegedly, his body was dumped at sea.

According to Iman, the palace at Bakara was rebuilt after the Padri Wars, only to be burned by the Dutch in 1878. Rebuilt once more, it was burned yet again by Dutch troops in 1883, following an unsuccessful raid on Baligé by the forces of King Sisingamangaraja XII.

Each time villages were destroyed, those people who could escape retreated north into the forest, returning later, gathering materials from the forest to rebuild.

The current Palace is a renovation carried out in 1978 by the Government of the Republic of Indonesia, with the local community. Iman pointed out that although the overall impression here was of real Batak houses, many details were not authentic. For example, there should be a meeting house and living houses, opposite grain stores, the two rows facing across a courtyard running East-West. Instead, the monuments occupy the space where the granaries should stand.

He pointed out details that he said were overlooked, such as how the rattan ropes that tie the roof to the walls should connect to a line, which, when released, would allow the whole roof to drop to the ground. This was a way to quickly put out a roof fire and prevent its spread to adjacent buildings. Here, that important detail had been omitted.

During the house building, he said, there were also many other protocols that should have been followed: ceremonies which were not carried out. But, in the end, he admitted, with a shrug, it is meaningful to have at least something here. A compromise, yet an important acknowledgement of such an important historical site.

Then he turned to the imagery used in the carvings. There are some common themes, he said, that we should be able to spot on other buildings if we looked for them. The house lizards, he explained, together with the nearby female breasts, represent fertility. The lizard can go anywhere, even upside down in the house. The Batak people can survive anywhere they might find themselves in the world, and maintain strong bonds, even when they meet in places far from their origins.

The grasshopper, said Iman, is inscrutable. You cannot tell his expression. He looks the same in life as in death.

The house shape itself, he pointed out, is like a chicken, with its head and tail held high, and represents the warmth and shelter the chicken offers to her chicks, who shelter underneath. When the chicks run to the warmth and protection of the mother, they tuck in underneath the feathers at the front, under her breast, where they are hidden, warm and safe. Iman pointed out how the ladder leads up under the front of the building and in through a trapdoor. In other houses it reaches up to a small door at the front beneath the overhanging eaves

Traditional houses use no nails. Everything is tenon-jointed or tied. This makes the structure stable in earthquakes and makes it possible to take apart and move a house. Up on stilts, it is out of reach of any flooding. The stilts themselves are raised above the ground on rocks, to keep the ends from rotting.

14. Dugouts

As we sauntered down the steps from the palace at Lumban Raja toward the road, I asked Iman what he knew of the lake paddling culture. He explained how the large solus, *solus bolon*, were essential for carrying people and goods before the Dutch built roads. Since then, there has been no need to connect by water.

"It's much easier to hop on a bus or ride a motorcycle to market nowadays than to travel by boat. If you need to cross to Sibandang or Samosir Island, there are plenty of motor ferries."

He confirmed that the solu was a small dugout, usually paddled solo. The solu bolon was a large one capable of carrying anything from twenty to fifty people. It could be from nine to thirty meters long (thirty to more than one hundred feet).

In 1883, when King Sisingamangaraja XII gathered forces to attack the Dutch, first at Laguboti, where they were successful, and later at Baligé, where they were not, part of his eight-thousand-strong force arrived in a battle fleet of forty to fifty solus bolon. Such a flotilla of sizable dugouts must have presented an imposing sight, but what kind of timber was used for such large boats, and where was it found?

The tree of choice was most likely *Shorea meranti*. Meranti typically grows up to sixty meters tall (two hundred feet), in sixty years, with a trunk diameter of about 86cm (three feet). A log from such a tree would suffice for one solu bolon. But as we saw from the lake, the shores are steep grassland slopes, not forest. The forests were mostly inland on the higher ground. Any huge trees that once grew at the lakeside, or close to the top of the scarp, must have been cut long ago. Since then, it must have taken diplomacy and negotiation to access a suitable tree, and to transport the solu bolon past maybe hostile villages, across whatever the terrain, to reach the lake.

Recently, descendants of King Simatupang, from the Muara district, midway between Baligé and Bakara in south Lake Toba, wished to build two solus bolon. They found trees big enough for the purpose, but they grew deep in the forest about sixty-five kilometers (forty miles) south of the lake. The family felled a total of seven meranti trees there in 2013, and were able to build two solus bolon, plus six small solus from the logs.

They carved the solus bolon and solus where the trees fell. Each solu bolon measured twenty-one meters long, 110cm wide, 70cm deep (68 feet long, three feet six inches wide, two feet four inches deep). In difficult terrain some ten kilometers (six miles) from the nearest road, the workers lashed a bamboo frame around each dugout to provide carrying handles. Having cut a path through the forest, they carried each canoe in turn down to the road by hand. As I understand it, 333 of the king's descendants shared this work. On reaching the road, the team continued to carry the boats all the way to Lake Toba in the traditional way. It cannot have been easy.

When the time was auspicious for launching, a large crowd gathered to watch. A melody floated in the air from a sarune bolon, a traditional clarinet-style double reed wind instrument, while each solu bolon was lifted and moved by hand, step by step down a ramp built at the shore and onto the water. The six smaller solus were launched too. The paddlers embarked, one into each solu and about twenty-three into each solu bolon, and the flotilla paddled out onto the lake. Everything from locating the trees to launching the finished craft was carried out in as similar a manner to the traditional way as possible.

15. Sacred Cave

With dusk fast approaching, we visited the sacred cave Tombak Sulusulu, where Boru Pasaribu gave birth to the child who was to become the first King Sisingamangaraja. Her pregnancy is said to have lasted for two years. At least she was in relative isolation for that long. The cave is set back from a high edge, overlooking the valley stretching down to the lake at Bakara.

The forest is called the Spear of Sulusulu, or the *light giver forest*. It is said that Boru Pasaribu saw lights spearing down into the forest here, maybe lightning. It is said that it was in the small cave in the forest, that she asked the creator god, *Mulajadi na Bolon*, for a son, since her husband had turned away from her after her daughter was born with a cleft palate.

The story tells how, when she gave birth after 2 years, her son already had teeth, a hairy tongue, and psychic gifts. When he grew up, he became the first King Sisingamangaraja.

There is a sign at the viewpoint, requesting respect and indicating where, in a shelter, to remove and leave shoes before walking onward barefoot. But there had been an earthquake here about ten years ago. When I followed the others in the half-light, I learned to my discomfort that since the earthquake, the soft earthen path to the cave had become a bed of sharp broken fragments of karst limestone. The way dropped steeply to the cave, so I scrambled awkwardly from one smooth exposed tree root to the next, trying to avoid the rock splinters.

The sacred cave was much bigger before, certainly large enough for Boru Pasaribu to live in, but it collapsed during the earthquake. What was left is rather low, more of a crawl space and diminished in area. It had an altar, which broke into two. Leaving the cave and continuing to use our headlamps in the gloom beneath the trees, we scrambled back up to find our shoes again.

Tombak Sulusulu sits on a step in the Bakara valley. From this vantage point we looked down along the green level-bottomed valley floor. The steep verdant slopes that climbed 450 meters either side of the valley (1,500 feet), framed a narrow view of Lake Toba.

Turning around at the same vantage point, we saw how up the valley small fields narrowed between the same steep slopes. A rushing river channeled toward us between neat banks. The valley appeared to dead-end after about a kilometer, taking an abrupt turn out of sight between the mountains. Somewhere around the corner, building commenced in 2017 on the Aek Silang 2 hydroelectric power plant. This was to harvest power from the water falling from the rim of the caldera. The river's nutrients have long been valuable to farmers in the valley, and now its energy has been utilized.

As daylight faded, lights appeared down in the valley. Standing talking with the three wise men, Iman, Saut and Tigor, I realized this might be the last time Tigor and Saut would be with us on our journey. We may see Tigor again, at the end of the trip, but regrettably not Saut.

I realized how Iman was revealing to me the cultural significance and rich historical value of Bakara and this valley. His knowledge ran deep. I had much to learn from him.

16. Mythology

In Batak mythology, there was a highest god who created the universe and everything in it. His name was *Debata (Ompung) Mulajadi na Bolon*. He created three levels of the world, the Upper Realm, Middle Earth, and the Underworld. He reigned in the sky, the upper realm, and ruled the middle world, and the underworld of spirits too, but he was known by different names in each of the three zones.

In the upper world he was called *Debata Mulajadi na Bolon*. In the middle world he was called *Silaon na Bolon*. In the spirit world, or underworld, he was known as *Pane na Bolon*.

His first creation was a chicken: the magical chicken called *Manukmanuk Hulambujati*. This blue chicken had an iron beak and skinny bracelet-clad claws.

Manukmanuk Hulambujati laid three eggs. These hatched into the gods *Debata Batara Guru*, *Debata Sori Sohaliapan*, and *Debata Bala Bulan*. Together these three were known as *Debata na Tolu*.

The daughter of Debata Batara Guru, *Si Boru Deak Parujar*, (*Sideak Parujar* is just one of her alternative names) was a weaver. She was the first spiritual creature to descend to earth, to the mountain Pusuk Buhit. On earth, she married her cousin, *Raja Odapodap,* who had changed his appearance, having earlier looked like a lizard.

Sideak Parujar and Raja Odapodap had a child shaped like an egg, and Debata Mulajadi na Bolon, the creator, told them to bury it. From that child sprouted all the plants of the earth.

Next, they gave birth to twins, one male and one female. These were named *Raja Ihat Manisia* and *Boru Ihat Manisia*. When they grew up, they married, and their children gave rise to all humans. Sideak Parujar and Raja Odapodap then both returned to the upper realm, and the connection between the upper realm and earth was broken, leaving the world to develop.

So, all the plants on earth, and the ancestor of the Batak people, *Si Raja Batak*, were the children of Sideak Parujar and Raja Odapodap.

There are many versions of this story, probably because the story was passed down as part of an oral tradition before ever being written. Here are some more details that commonly feature in the story.

Sideak Parujar had a reason for coming down to earth. Her older sister was intended to marry Raja Odapodap, but he was lizard-like, and she found him repulsive. At first, she refused, but the family pressure on her to accept was so great that she eventually went ahead with the ceremonies until, when the sun rose, she leaped from up high and disappeared down into the ground and vanished. Over time she emerged as the sugar palm tree.

This recalls the story Syahrul told me when we walked across the rice fields early in the trip.

Sideak Parujar, as the younger sister, was expected to substitute in the arranged marriage. But she made other plans. She spun a thread and used it to escape, descending from the upper realm, the sky, to the middle world.

Finding that the middle world was only water, she asked her great-grandfather, the creator, Debata Mulajadi na Bolon, for help. He sent her a handful of earth which she spread out to make land. She did not realize that she had spread it over the head of a monster, the dragon *Naga Padoha*, who lived in the underworld, and the dragon was annoyed.

Naga Padoha rolled and twisted, trying to dislodge the earth, which made things uncomfortable for Sideak Parujar. To subdue him she plunged her sword into him, up to the hilt. Then she clamped him in irons to immobilized him. She was successful at keeping him still, at least for the most part, for it is only occasionally that he shifts in his irons and then the earth shakes.

Sideak Parujar's lizard-like suitor saw where she had gone. In disguise he followed her down to earth, where she married him. The couple had twins, a boy, and a girl. Once the children were grown, both Sideak Parujar and Raja Odapodap returned to the upper realm, and the doorway to Middle Earth was closed.

The children, happy together, had an incestuous relationship, and their human children have since populated the earth. The couple settled at the foot of the volcano Pusuk Buhit, on the shore of Lake Toba, founding the village of Sianjur Mulamula. One of their children, *Si Raja Batak* is the mythological ancestor of the Batak people.

The Batak grew and divided into groups, each with its own cultural identity. The Toba Batak is one of those groups, the one we were interested to study on this trip, but there are others. The Angkola, Karo, Mandailing, Pakpak and Simalungun, occupy a wide area around the lake, as we saw at the museum in Baligé.

Each Batak group, in its own region, has its own variation of tradition, for example in architecture, language and religion, but there is much commonality of culture and ancestral beliefs. Some Batak groups have become primarily Muslim, or largely Protestant Christian, yet animist beliefs and adat, or custom law, still underlie the values of these more recently introduced religions.

Lake Toba is predominantly Protestant Christian at more than 90 percent, in a country with the largest Muslim population in the world.

Stepping back a little to consider Batak culture in the arena of Indonesia is rather like viewing a pine plantation from a distance. If there is anything else growing there, it is hidden beneath the canopy.

That canopy is Javanese. Java dominates Indonesia economically, politically, and culturally, so at a casual glance everything across Indonesia appears consistent and uniform. It appears Javanese. But there are myriad other cultures across Indonesia.

Rather than spreading a monoculture pine forest, it could be better to let a more species-diverse forest grow, one that showcases the individuality of each kind of tree without hiding it beneath the canopy. No matter if some cultures are more ancient than others, the unique combination would be richer for all.

As we returned from Tombak Sulusulu toward Bakara, the car's headlights burning the dark as we dropped into the valley, we stopped at a house surrounded by small farming plots. Light streamed welcoming from the windows. Pak Uli ran inside. This was where he lived, and he would be leaving home for a few more days to come with us.

17. Breezy

When I awoke in the big room, Harriet was still sleeping, Ade was motionless, and Tandon and Ally had not yet emerged from their room. A loose metal sheet somewhere behind the house was still banging loudly against the wall in the wind. It had been beating throughout the night, and evidently the conditions had not eased.

Greeting us in the semidarkness, Tandon threw open the window shutters to let in full daylight. Moments later they slammed shut again at him with a force that would have shattered the glass panes, had there been any. I wondered if the wind would affect our paddling plans.

At the back of the house, stepped down to ground level from the meeting room, was the kitchen. There to my left on the counter I saw a single big gas burner, with a huge pot of water already on to heat. On my right, screened off by a low internal wall from the rest of the kitchen, was the bathroom. Behind the barrier, a big tank of water stood in the corner, with a long-handled scoop to use for flushing the hole-in-the-floor toilet and for washing and showering. As usual, there was no toilet paper, but plenty of water instead. On one occasion in conversation, someone asked innocently whether water was expensive in America. "No, not where we live. Not unless you want to buy it in a bottle. Why?"

"I wondered why you would waste paper if there was water available?"

The whole floor drained to one corner, where there was an outlet. With the entire floor always awash and only one tiny shelf off the floor, it was all too easy to emerge after a shower with wet clothing. I needed to take more care.

There was no running water, at least not this morning. In the past, villages were built near a spring or near the lake. Fresh water for cooking and drinking was brought to the house in a ceramic pot carried on the head, but there would be no toilet in the house. Any washing or bathing would be done in the lake, or at another water source if the lake were too distant.

Here, we were just a short walk from the lake, yet there was a lot of water in the tank in the bathroom. When kayaking we had already passed numerous white plastic pipes running uphill from the lake, and it is these pipes that nowadays carry lake water to the houses, using a gasoline-powered pump to top up the water levels when necessary.

"How do you think the lake will be, with all this wind?" asked Kristin. "Do you think it will affect us?"

"I don't know," I replied. But curious, I offered, "I'll come with you if you'd like to find out."

We grabbed our shoes and stepped outside. It was only a short distance to walk, straight down the road past the traditional Batak houses and the few small newer buildings. A big tree stood at the end of the road, with the lake just beyond. But our way appeared blocked.

In the middle of the road, beside a stack of white sacks, two men were winnowing rice onto a big tarp. The winnowing machine was crudely constructed from timber and plywood, with carrying handles at each end, all painted rust-red and white. It was powered by a little gasoline engine mounted to the side, its fuel tank on the top. Belts ran to the driveshaft. A man dressed in a blue plaid shirt and long pants, with a black baseball cap pulled low over his head, poured rice from a large white sack into the hopper at the top. A second man, in sweatshirt, shorts, and with bare feet, used a long-handled wooden hoe to drag the rice away as it fell through the bottom of the winnower. He spread the rice across the huge tarp. Already heavily weighed down with mounds of rice, the tarp, pinned at the edges with rocks, stretched wider than the road.

From the back end of the winnower spat the ejected husks and fragments of stalk and debris gathered with the harvest. This piled up onto a small blue tarp. The air was loud with clatter and full of flying dust from the husks, and with exhaust fumes from the motor.

We skirted narrowly between the building and the edge of the tarp and past the café, today closed. There were the tidily stacked kayaks where the café owners had invited Priyo, Swina, and Kristin to leave them last night, just beyond the beach.

The lake was embroidered with the bright flash of breakers, the strongest gusts of wind rasping up dark patches of frenzy. A cloud of egrets, brilliant white in the sunlight, drifted against the sky.

At our feet, plastic lay strewn deeply across the beach. There were all kinds of bottles and lightweight single-use cups with straws. It was the kind of debris that could have floated in and washed up here, accumulating into this deep layer or caught at the edge by the water hyacinth. There did not appear to be any garbage that might sink.

I had not seen a beach on Lake Toba with so much rubbish as this. Did certain lake beaches naturally collect debris, just as some ocean beaches collect driftwood while others nearby always stay clean? On the ocean it is the tides, currents and winds that decide. Here, I could trace its origin if I knew the prevailing wind direction. The garbage was mostly near the shoreline. Turning, I could see a partly filled wheelbarrow at the top of the beach, where the raked ground showed that someone cared to clean up.

A sarcophagus towered behind the beach. On the top of the main edifice stood a large model of a building in the shape of a saddleback house. It was painted creamy yellow and blue, with a black roof, the pale jawbone of a buffalo displayed at its balcony where drums might hang. The sun lit this colorful monument into dramatic contrast against a patch of dark slate-grey sky.

Priyo and the others joined us for breakfast. Coffee came from the kitchen, where the big pot of water had finally boiled, but when breakfast came, it was bustled in through the front door. Other women had prepared and cooked it elsewhere. The dishes were displayed in the center of the meeting room floor on the mats, where everyone could serve themselves. Along with a small bowl of water for each of us to rinse our fingers, there was the usual menu of rice, sambals, eggs, chicken and fish, the latter today being little bony fish. It made a sustaining breakfast.

The primary ingredients for our meals were the same from one day to the next, and from one meal to the next, but meals were offered to us visitors as a group. It is more usual here for food to be prepared each morning for the entire family for the whole day. Each person helps themselves to food when they need it rather than sitting together as a family for meals. Our lunch was prepared with our breakfast, for us to take with us, but since we were traveling, our evening meal would be cooked later, somewhere else.

We ate sitting on the floor, either with fingers, or with a fork and spoon, but as people moved around or reached for rice, or for another egg, they swung a hand or leg behind to prop for balance. This led to some spillage of tea and coffee. It was challenging to find a safe place to stand a cup. Thankfully, the floor mat where I sat was coffee colored.

We had slept on these same mats, which were spread out for us last night, with our Thermarest mattresses on top, with pillows and blankets provided by our hosts. Our own mats, not strictly necessary, covered the cracks between the planks where the wind blows through, even when covered by the thin floor mats. It made me appreciate the design practicalities of the houses here.

Traditionally a house is built high above the ground on stilts with plenty of airflow under the floor. The breeze blows up through the cracks between the floorboards, keeping the house cool. With no ceiling to block the high roof, hot air is free to rise and escape through the substantially vented outward-sloping front and rear walls. Dust falls through the cracks or is easily swept into them if not gathered up.

This house, although raised only a little above the ground and despite its lower ceiling, still enabled airflow. A breeze came through the cracks between the floorboards. The windows without glass allowed hot air to rise and escape. The woven plastic mats we sat on to eat, and slept on, were only spread out for the occasion, and were otherwise rolled up.

With breakfast over, and everything cleared away, we sat together around the map. Priyo pointed out our route ahead, and the location of places of interest that we should visit. Today we would aim for a place that was not marked on the map. "It's somewhere around here," he said, his slender finger circling vaguely. "It's twenty kilometers, roughly twelve miles. I should recognize it when we get there. Swina will be waiting."

When Syahrul brought his pickup truck to collect us and carry us and our gear to our kayaks to launch, Kristin and Priyo walked the shorter distance to theirs. We would meet again on the water. There, waiting for the others, we paddled constantly just to keep place against the wind. After a while, Kristin and I decided to cross the bay, two kilometers (a mile) to wait in the shelter of Simamora Island instead.

***

There are only a handful of islands within Lake Toba, its shores generally too steep and deep. This one, fewer than four hundred meters long (a quarter mile) appeared to be uninhabited. We tucked out of the wind behind its steep hill, drifting in warm sunshine at the edge of a shelf of water hyacinth that clung to the island. Bushes defended the shore and the lower slope, some spangled with bright yellow flowers. In places, trees punctured this dense cover, thrusting up through the barrier. Above, the green hill opened steeply, clad in lush knee-deep vegetation. Birds sang and insects darted through the air.

Priyo approached, paddling purposefully alongside Saleh, his metallic green whitewater helmet on his head not for protection, but to head-mount his video camera. Behind him the steep green scarp of the caldera towered like a wall.

A jumbling flock of white egrets flew in toward the island, with a pair of what appeared to be purple herons in their midst. They all gathered at the windy north end of the island, alighting onto and relaunching from a large mango tree. They seemed uncertain whether to stop or not.

When they approached the tree to land, their flying seemed precarious, a successful landing always in doubt. Their huge wings twisted and trembled, jolted and juddered by the wind, long legs stretched down. One by one they settled, until the tree was coated completely white. One by one we too gathered.

"Look over there!" I pointed as our boat, arriving from the south with the last of our group, cut its engines to drift toward us. "Look! A rare example of a white mango tree. Have you ever seen one of those?"

Tandon shook his head, humoring me, then leaning from the boat he waved a packet of cookies enticingly in the air. He drew us all together as surely as if he had hooked us on a line. We passed the carton back and forth, from kayak to kayak, until it was empty. Although it was already some time since we launched, any decisive move to depart appeared unlikely. Eventually it took a little tugging at the edge of the group to ease it gently from inertia.

Sliding quietly past the white mango tree, we bucked a headwind to the next resting place, behind a narrow finger of land. Then we forged on hard until we had fully left Bakara Bay, when the paddling became easier and the scenery increasingly dramatic. Steep sweeping ramps of lush green foliage dropped to the water's edge in splatters of golden yellow flowers, purple morning glories, and clumps of what looked like white umbellifers.

Individual pines stood out on the steep grassy slopes, and mango trees edged the shoreline. Sometimes, as we paddled intimately close to the shore, we were startled by grey water buffalo standing in or at the edge of the water. These were sometimes hidden by the undergrowth until we were almost within touching distance. It was a shock to be suddenly so close to something so large, with long curving horns, but thankfully they seemed placid and not inclined to panic.

Brilliant flashes of iridescent blue, sometimes just a flash caught from the corner of the eye, turned out to be kingfishers speeding in a straight-line past. They always seemed purposeful, heading directly toward a target, but then seemed to vaporize, their disappearance being so abrupt and complete. When we neared the place where they had disappeared, they would burst into view again like a shooting star, speeding away in a blaze of shining blue, following the shoreline.

Overhead a Brahminy kite, *Haliastur indus,* wandered casually, hanging lazily on the wind, watching. The Brahminy kite is the Garuda, the national emblem of Indonesia.

Beneath the kayaks, goldfish, or carp, about twenty centimeters long (nine inches) and gleaming orange, swam in the shallows, undisturbed by us drifting overhead. Along the shore, fishermen were spaced respectfully apart along the bank. Others sat with rod and line in small wooden dugout solus, or plastic versions of them, anchored by the water hyacinth.

There were no buildings, at least none were visible between the shoreline and the steep slopes immediately behind. But there were people here, perhaps dropped off by boat. Men and women gathered mangoes from the mature trees that grew all along at the shore. Some had climbed the trees and were mostly hidden in the foliage. Had they not called out, "Horas! Horas! Horas!" we might not have seen them, being distracted instead by those on the ground beneath the trees, busy filling deep baskets.

In places, trees grew so close to the steep shore that it would be impossible for us to reach land through the tangle of dangling creepers and roots. They had grown together into dense natural nets. In other places, tall thick undergrowth would have prevented us from landing. Wherever the water was sheltered, a skirt of water hyacinth guarded the shore.

The steep slopes rising into the foliage also sank steeply underwater. Looking down past one side of my kayak, I saw it to be dramatically shallower than on the other side, even though my kayak was narrow. If on one side I could stand to my knees in water, I would swim out of my depth on the other.

Paddling around the little points of land that jutted out into the lake, I felt the bottom-drag of the shallows resist my push forwards for just a moment. A single paddle stroke more and my hull released, floating freely over deep water again. I looked up. High in the dip of the hills stood a solitary concave-ridged building, a distant observer, a saddle shape within the saddle.

I sped around a corner through a gap between a rock and the shore and quite unexpectedly ran into our escort boat. There it floated, colorful as a clown right in front of me, moored to the steep rock in the shelter of the cliff. It was in a perfectly sheltered pool of deep clear water. Ally stood long-legged on the paddle board. Harriet swam, luxuriating in the warm water, while Tandon floated like a sea otter, busy with his waterproof camera at his chest. The others hailed us from the boat, their greetings echoing from the cliff.

"Here! We have your packed lunches!"

They reached down to hand them out. Then we sat on our kayaks with our feet dangling in the water, pulling fingerfuls of rice, fish, and sambal, from the leaf wrappers. Iman passed us fresh cut avocado. It was a tasty meal, if a little awkward to handle balanced like that. Yet nothing was wasted. Any morsel dropped into the clear water was snatched up by darting fish.

Continuing our way, hugging the shore, we passed houses, and villages. Here a jumble of rust-red roofs sheltered between palms and bananas and mango trees. There a saddleback shape, like a house, formed the top tier of a hillside tomb. The fiery red blossoms of a tree blazed amid the tangle of shrubs and pines. Behind soared the steep grassland slopes, peppered with trees, rising to six hundred meters (2,000 feet) above the lake. The slopes were slashed by the deep V-cuts of drainage gullies and an occasional raw landslip gash. Down into an interlock of V-shaped valleys fell a silver-white torrent, a long waterfall so powerful I could almost feel its thunder in my bones and its cool spray on my skin.

There were dry riverbeds too. The jumble of big, rounded boulders, the headroom under the bridges, plus the height of the containing walls, all hinted at the volume of water that must sometimes rage down. Yet the lake plunged so steeply from the shore that these rivers could scarcely form deltas. At one outlet, a field of pale boulders some seventy meters wide (eighty yards) marked the end of a river that could run for no more than three kilometers (two miles) dropping from the caldera rim 1,200 meters above us (4,000 feet). This river would erupt into flash floods and soon dry, for the watershed follows the caldera edge. Rain falling outside the rim drains south toward Bakara.

Paddling onward we saw bigger boats, both tourist vessels and ferries, parked bow to shore. The tourist boats were multi-decked with colorful paint jobs. I noticed panels painted to look like wooden beams where the superstructure been built less solidly. A crowd of young boys watched silently from the top of an old boat, while men shouted, "Horas!"

There were more solus too, constructed from blue plastic drums. Pinched together at one end to form the bow, the split drums were opened enough to insert wooden ribs inside. A straight beam attached underneath served as a keel, and wooden boards were added as gunnel strips. Most were equipped with a small inboard motor, and care had been taken when pulling ashore to protect the little propeller by propping the boat on a log or stone with the stern raised. A group of young men by the shore said they had built their own plastic barrel solus. They posed proudly in them, brandishing fish harpoons and spearguns, snorkels and goggles.

Half an hour later we reached a shrine close to the water's edge. A few steps led up to the entrance of an enclosure, in which a roof sheltered a white-painted rock shaped like a wave and a symbolic solu. There was a sign reading something like; *Guru Sonungdangon Borun Saroding's*... and the text ran on, possibly in Toba Batak, for Priyo, Indonesian from Java, could not understand it. Toba Batak is an Austronesian language still spoken by about two million people around the Lake Toba area. It was at first written in Batak script, although Roman script has become more usual, as on this sign.

A man walking along the track hailed us as he approached, to request that we did not enter the enclosure. It seems the shrine is a place where people prayed for a safe crossing to Samosir Island, and it was associated with a woman. Above stood a huge tree, which had shed some substantial limbs onto another building inside the enclosure and crumpled the fence.

Later I uncovered the story behind the shrine. It concerns a beautiful and talented woman who came from Samosir Island, from a huta near Mogang on the peninsula, the closest point of land on Samosir from here. While she bathed in the lake one day, and washed her hair, a boat approached her. In it she saw a handsome, well-built man not dressed as a fisherman.

Her parents and two brothers liked the man too, so after some time the couple married and she returned with him to his home in the forest at Ulu Darat, near the mountain peak of Rassang Bosi, right across the water from where her parents lived. There one day, she saw a huge snake in the tree by the house, with a strange head, and suspected that when her husband left the house, he turned into a snake.

When she confronted him about it, he admitted it was true. She seemed to accept it, which reassured him. So, when she later said she would like to visit her parents, he reluctantly agreed to let her go. He accompanied her to the lake shore, where he made her promise that she would return. She swore an oath that she would come back to him or come to harm if she broke her promise.

Sadly, he watched from the shore as his wife paddled her solu toward Samosir Island. When she was far from land, she declared that since her husband was not human, that he was really a snake, she would never return. Within moments the sky grew dark and the waves kicked up. Terrified, she kept on paddling, but the waves finally tipped her over and she drowned. A shrine was built here in her memory. The place she drowned was named Paranggir-anggiran ni si boru Saroding.

Finally, we reached a resort. The fancy complex of square ocher-yellow hotel buildings, almost apricot, stood three storeys high with railed balconies and big glazed windows. It seemed incongruous here, so modern, and comparatively big. It was grandly terraced up from the water, standing above three layers of concrete walls and terraces. The lowest terrace was decorated with potted plants, the middle level provided with benches. Behind the hotel rose a steep green valley in the caldera scarp. I wondered how quickly Lake Toba waterfront will become developed.

Here for the night, we lifted our kayaks up the steps to leave on the middle terrace. The cavernous Hadorassa Resort was a new place, at most two or three years old. Swina greeted us, excited to show us around. Handing us our room key, she led us upstairs. Unusually, each flight had a constant step height until the final significantly taller step. Either the architect or the builder had miscalculated. At the third and top floor, Swina stepped aside with a flourish, smiling to welcome us into our luxury room. There, a mirror floor of immaculate stone tiles spread to a balcony with a clear view east-southeast down the lake.

18. Sitor's Poetry

I joined Iman on the terrace over late afternoon coffee to hear about his father and forebears. Iman's father, Sitor Situmorang, had published numerous books, some of poems, more of short stories, yet others about Toba Batak village life and structure, and Indonesian history. He had also written about his own father, Iman's grandfather, brother-in-law of King Sisingamangaraja XII.

The Situmorang clan were wife-givers to the Sisingamangarajas. According to Toba Batak adat, the custom law, there should be a strong tie within a group of three clans, each clan giving daughters for marriage into one, and receiving daughters for marriage from the other. The wife giver clan was referred to by the wife receiver clan as the hula-hula. As hula-hula, members of the Situmorang clan were held in the highest esteem by the Sisingamangarajas.

Iman opened his bag and pulled out some copies of his father's books in Bahasa Indonesia, the official Indonesian language. These, he said, as he straightened them on the table in front of him, he brought as gifts for the Indonesians in our group. To Harriet he gave Sitor's book of poems, *To Love, To Wander,* the English translation by John H McGlynn. With a new cover, it was a later edition than the one Kristin and I had brought with us. (The Lontar Foundation, Jakarta, 2014.)

As we sat eating dinner on the terrace, I watched the view across the lake to the southeast slowly change. The sun dropped behind the mountains behind us, and the light soon faded until I could no longer see a horizon between the black water and the black sky. The only hint of a dividing line was the appearance of a few lights on nearby Samosir Island, *Pulau Samosir*. All color had vanished, yet lingering in my mind, like an afterglow, was the image of the high green curve of the caldera with its steep rim, and at the water's edge the walls of exposed igneous gabbro and andesite rock that geologist Saleh had pointed out.

I might have been aware of a difference in the appearance of the types of rock, without ever questioning the reason. It took Saleh's explanation for me to see it. Although the dark colored gabbro has the same chemical composition as basalt, it is more granular in structure, the effect of the long period of cooling deep underground which allows crystals to grow. On a geological timescale, basalt cools quickly, gabbro slowly.

Andesite also an igneous rock but with a different mineral content from gabbro, cools quickly like basalt before any granular structure can form. It is extruded at convergent plate margins, and is particularly associated with subduction zones, like here along the Sumatran fault.

Sated from dining, yet idly picking at the remains of dinner, we drank tuak while Iman read out loud one of his father's poems, in Bahasa Indonesia. It was about Lake Toba and as if in sympathy with his reading the wind sprang up, the air chilled and my skin prickled. When Priyo began to translate the gist of it for us, it began to rain.

We carried the chairs into the shelter of the foyer, where Kristin read aloud the English translation of the poem, *Lake Toba's Topography*, from *To Love, To Wander*. I felt Sitor's love of his homeland by the lake. Kristin read on,

> ... *From one side to the other, mountain forests hold*
> *fast the valleys of mother nature's heart, the blue and*
> *peaceful waters in the midst of the world's clamor...*

Reading Sitor's poetry with Kristin before we arrived at Lake Toba, helped us see the lake from the perspective of someone who clearly loved it. Yet his vantage point was that of someone who had spent most of his life away, thinking often about his ancestral home.

His writing struck a chord with me. I travel a lot, and often miss my home in Seattle, but that home too is far from my family and my country of birth. Sitor conveys well in his writings those feelings of separation and longing, tugging against an urge to travel and explore. Those moments of reflection while staying in an impersonal room somewhere, on the way from, and on the way to, other transitory havens.

People, a suitcase, a chance meeting that glimmers and evaporates, a love lost, a missed opportunity. Never quite at home when away. And then, once having been away, never quite at home when returned.

We were still there in the foyer, late, when Syahrul arrived with Indra Hidayatwas. To our disappointment, Pindi Setiawan was not with them. Apparently, he was ill with either Dengue fever or malaria and was awaiting test results. Both Indra and Pindi belong to the mountain and jungle exploration association, Wanadri, and both are from the Institut Teknologi Bandung.

Pindi is a researcher from the art faculty, where he is an expert on prehistoric cave paintings. I had looked forward to meeting him and learning something of the history of the ancient artwork that Nicklas Millegård, of Millekul Adventures, showed me on the sea cliffs of Misool, West Papua.

A visit to study Misool was on Pindi's schedule for later this month. There, some of the ocher handprints and painted images date back thousands of years. Could he discern how they came to be? For example, had they been painted like signposts on the exposed cliffs, or were they painted deep in caves, only becoming exposed as the sea eroded the cliffs?

Misool is more than 3,500km away (2,200 miles) from Lake Toba, but there is evidence of humans here on Sumatra too, dating back between 73,000 and 63,000 years. That evidence came from the analysis of teeth found in Lida Ajer, a limestone cave near Mount Sago in the Padang Highlands, West Sumatra, 350 kilometers (220 miles) from here. The dating coincides with Northern Australian human artifacts from 65,000 years ago.

A route from Africa to Australia at that time would have looked quite different from nowadays, with the sea level much lower. In the Pleistocene epoch, the islands of Sumatra, Java and Borneo would have been joined as part of mainland Southeast Asia, known as the continent of Sunda. Australia, Papua, and Tasmania together would have made another single land mass, Sahul.

In the mid-1800s, the British naturalist, Alfred Russel Wallace, observed the species barrier remaining between what had been the two land masses, separated by a strait, now called the Wallace Line. Common species found across Sunda were absent from Sahul, and vice versa.

But distances of up to twenty-four kilometers (fifteen miles) across water seem to have been no insurmountable barrier to early hominids, who reached the island of Flores. The small hominid, Homo floresiensis, is thought to have lived on Flores from around 95,000 years ago until about 17,000 years ago, and it is not thought there was any land bridge that could have made that island accessible. Reaching it along the island chain must, it seems, have been by boat or raft, the technology required to reach Australia.

It is interesting to note that although much of the period when these little hominids occupied Flores was prior to the eruption of Toba, they were still there afterwards, so they must have survived it. The wind direction during the eruption may have spared them by carrying most of the ash west toward India and Africa.

If people migrated across Sunda it is most likely they occupied the coastal areas, which have since been flooded by the rising sea level. If so, the most likely locations for cave art may now be submarine. But that does not preclude the possibility of cave art here on higher ground too. After all, there are limestone caves, even around Lake Toba, and hematite deposits which could have been utilized as pigment. Ancient hominid remains have been found in Sumatra. Unfortunately, the questions I had for Pindi would have to wait. I hoped he would make a swift recovery.

When I asked Syahrul about his day, he said his drive had been challenging. Having collected Indra, the GPS on his phone led him over the mountains on narrow roads, with steep drops, hairpin turns, and poor road quality. It was a terrible route. In the end he turned around and went back, starting over again on a big circuitous route around the mountains instead. Alas, he admitted, he had bashed in the front corner of his car in the mountains.

19. Cobra

Kristin and I awoke to the dawn with an unbroken view from the third floor across the calm lake, where white egrets drifted in the air. In the distance, a bubble of cumulus cloud, edged in silver, sprouted from a bank of grey cloud. Around it, a pale peach-colored glow prepared the blue sky for the arrival of the sun. Looking down from the balcony, I spotted Tandon striding around. He was already busy scoping out the terrace for the best camera angle for the sunrise. Shortly, we joined him there for coffee and then for breakfast.

When I launched, I drifted, waiting for everyone else to get ready, taking a moment to relax and absorb the scene. An elderly man tended his garden just along the shore from the hotel. The land there was banked up in terraces. I watched him move stiffly from his house along a terrace, between the foliage of his crops, checking and inspecting, stooping with difficulty.

Standing in the shallows at the water's edge, an elderly woman, maybe his wife, hitched up her sarong to bend over her task, washing clothes in the lake.

We were in the noticeably narrowing channel between the mainland shore, along which we explored, and Samosir Island. Small ferries hovered at the shore for trucks and cars to board. I watched one ferry speed to reach land. The moment the ramp dropped; two cars disembarked onto the dirt beach. With engines alternately racing and laboring, they crawled slowly up a bumpy track in low gear.

Now a short yellow and green bus boarded. Half-filling the ferry, it stopped when it reached the balance-point midway. Just moments later, the ramp lifted, and the ferry pulled away from shore again in a cloud of dark smoke, reversing and turning hard. The bow swinging quickly around, the engines paused for a moment and then gunned into forward gear. The ferry sped off, aiming for Samosir Island just a few hundred meters away. It was a short crossing, served by a whole fleet of these tiny ferries.

I coughed, but it was not just the exhaust from the ferry that troubled my breathing. Bonfires burned all along the shore today. Some were burning brush, piles of cleared vegetation like the stalks of rice or maize. Other piles of waste from small-scale farming burned plastic too, emanating a dark cloying sooty smoke that rasped in my throat. The air all around was hazy, softening detail and obscuring the distant view.

Turning my attention from the shore, I saw numerous floating platforms of water hyacinth drifting in the opposite direction to me, encouraged along by a slight breeze. Water hyacinth was introduced here in the 1960s and 1970s as a source of fiber for baskets and bags but as far as I know never seriously exploited.

Water hyacinth fibers are quite strong, so they are often used just as they are. Otherwise, they are twisted into a stronger twine or yarn for fabric or braided. They can also be used in conjunction with rattan to make furniture. Rattan, a native species, is one of Indonesia's biggest exports, already widely exploited to make furniture. A frame is constructed from rattan poles, with rattan core added for thinner supports, and woven into panels for tabletops, seat backs and cushions. Water hyacinth fibers can be woven onto a rattan frame instead to create a softer finish.

In other applications water hyacinth is processed to blend with fibers of polyester, wool, or cotton, for household and clothing textiles. It is also woven into shoe soles and mats, incorporated into fiberboard, and used for stuffing upholstery. However promising, little if any use of it is made here yet. Not that all its useful properties are seen after it is harvested. Alive, it not only filters heavy metals from the water, but also nitrogen and phosphorus, two major nutrient loads associated with aquaculture: effluent from fish farms is currently overburdening Lake Toba. Water enriched with phosphorus and nitrogen can lead to algal blooms and a drop in oxygen levels, something that has already resulted in fish deaths on a massive scale at some of Lake Toba's fish farms.

So, to a point, water hyacinth could mitigate by absorbing excess nitrogen and phosphorus, so long as it is adequately controlled. But once water hyacinth blankets the water, it blocks sunlight from the native water plants that normally keep the water oxygenated. At that point it can deplete oxygen levels and cause its own fish deaths. The floating blankets are also ideal breeding grounds for mosquitoes.

Water hyacinth is a known invasive species. Here I saw it mostly just around the edges of the lake. Could it really become a problem, after all Lake Toba is a big lake? Yes, water hyacinth has the potential to scale up to create serious problems.

Undisturbed and in ideal conditions, a single water hyacinth plant, costing on average about US $6 on eBay, could in theory produce 28,000 tons of fresh plant material in just one year. Under good conditions it can double its mass every four days. It already carpets much of Africa's largest manmade reservoir, Lake Kariba and clogs the turbines of its hydroelectric plants. Fishermen struggle to find any way to access open water on Lake Victoria, Africa's biggest lake. It is thought to have been introduced into Africa in the nineteenth century by Belgian colonists, so it has had longer to proliferate. Those who care about Lake Toba's future would do well to learn from how Africans are tackling their new reality, and to do so soon.

At one recess into the Toba shore, water hyacinth grew like a shelf from the cliff into a gently undulating carpet. Curious to find out how easily I could push through, I accelerated up to full speed and rammed into it. I was stopped abruptly. Little more than my bow had penetrated the dense mass. It was deeper and much more interwoven than I had ever imagined.

But out here, away from shore, the crisp vegetation looked cheerfully decorative. Small floating bright green islands crept caterpillar-like on the waves, crawling away to find new territory. White egrets dropped like paper in the wind and folded themselves onto the rafts, finding refuge safely distant from the shore.

Not all the floating platforms I passed here were green and natural. Many were man-made, anchored or staked in position to prevent them drifting away. Nets strung between blue plastic drums formed holding tanks for fish. Netted over as well as underneath, they denied the ubiquitous herons and egrets an easy meal. The plastic drums used as floats were of the same kind that locals cut up for canoe construction.

A man energetically shoveling with a flat green plate to bail his boat, called "Horas!" to us as we passed. We greeted him in return, and he stopped bailing to paddle along with us. I drew closer alongside and we paused to compare paddles. Then he proudly showed us the crayfish he had collected from his pots. This being one of the shallower areas of the lake at less than fifty meters (160 feet), it must be easier to set pots here than in the deeper parts which plunge to more than five hundred meters. Now Ade passed us, standing on his paddle board. Seeing him, the fisherman jumped to his feet and set off in pursuit. Challenged into standing in my kayak, I realized I was not nearly as balanced as he was.

The fisherman kept pace with us for a while, but when I sat down again, he sat too, drifting to a standstill to resume bailing. Edging his canoe, he scooped vigorously with his plate to splash out the water. Meanwhile he maintained stability with his paddle held in his other hand. His boat appeared to be made from metal oil drums, flattened, and paneled onto a frame, in much the same way that plastic drums were bent to a frame. Ostensibly it was a canoe, both in design and in the way he paddled it, and his paddle was long in the shaft like some of the others we had seen. It was a good length to use while standing, yet he was the first person I saw to use it like that. We left him bailing and pressed on after Ade.

Kingfishers flashed in the sun. They seemed to be everywhere along the shore here, catching my attention with a spark of brightness and then defying my eye to follow the arrow flight. I was delightfully distracted by them, paddling alongside Kristin just a little ahead of the others. But shortly after we passed the narrowest point between the mainland and Samosir Island, Priyo called us back to where some ferries landed. Iman had told a local family, descendants of Raja Tamba, that we would be passing, and they had kindly invited us to visit.

We lifted the kayaks clear of the shore and sealed the cockpits. From there, a long white concrete road ran up the hill past rice terraces. Chickens and ducks busily turned over leaves and probed beside the road, splashing through the mud pools between the rows of stiff rice plants.

In other fields the tufts of rice stood like the clumps of bristles studding a brush, while the sky reflected in the calm water between. We passed a tiny shop at a crossroads, with a jumble of motorcycles parked outside: a lunchtime gathering. Otherwise, there were just a few scattered houses, plots of maize, and clustered coffee bushes beside the rice fields. After five hundred meters (550 yards) where the road steepened and meandered, Iman stopped.

"Look," he said. "Bamboo." He pointed to a dense thicket of bamboo; six to nine meters tall (20-30 feet). The stems were as thick as my leg. He emphasized again its importance in protecting a huta and pointed out how in a heavily vegetated area, it would help hide any habitations. Not here, for although the buildings were hidden, the bamboo gave their location away.

We continued up the road to beyond the bamboo barrier and there was huta Tamba, and a beautiful chicken-shaped house built in the last century. It was one in a row of houses up there on the hill. The intricately carved wooden façade was decorated just here and there with a little red paint. With all the conversation in Bahasa Indonesia, Tandon translated what he overheard. "The red paint was once mixed using the blood taken from enemies."

We stood outside on the grassy yard to look at the building, our backs to a cliff of outcropping rock. Nagari Tamba, the first owner, built the house farther up the hill and it has been moved here since. The roof was neatly tiled using ornamental tiles, and steps in front of the house curved elegantly inward and upward to a short and narrow door.

To create more living space, the original house had been extended sideways by adding a lower, L-shaped, wooden-paneled house. This too had a clay-tiled roof. Beside the extension in the same row stood two more buildings with metal roofs, most likely for storage.

With the house in this new position someone calling from the little balcony at the front where ceremonial drums are sometimes mounted, could be heard in the open courtyard in front of the house. Cleverly, the message would also be heard far down in the valley behind; the sound reflecting out from the cliff opposite.

The carving on the house front was calming, pleasingly clean. Wondering what was different, I realized that most of the carvings here were around the edges in narrow borders, like carved hems. The hanging parts were not only surface-carved, but also cut through with decorative fretwork. Inscribed names and dates further personalized the façade. A date was chiseled: 1940.

We climbed up to the big meeting room, the single space in the original building, since linked at the side by stairs into the extension. Some of the little hatches, or window shutters, hung open to let the breeze and the sunlight stream in. There we were welcomed by Ompung Humisar boru Tamba, the youngest daughter of Raja Tamba, and Roy Tamba, grandson of Raja Tamba, and several young children.

Iman drew me aside to point out details I would have certainly missed. Up there, he indicated, the roof was held in place with stylish leather straps, not rattan ropes. Here and there, carefully incised carvings decorated the timbers. Intricately shaped corbels capped the posts where they supported the roof.

"See how the wood has been prepared?" The surface of the timbers had been planed smooth. That clean modern-style treatment revealed its more recent provenance. Timbers in older buildings were shaped using an adze. Smooth planks lined the inside of the roof, the red wood casting down a warm glow. Ordinarily the structural poles and struts supporting the roof would be visible.

To prepare the room for us, huge woven plastic mats were carefully unrolled across the floor, one in purple and yellow, decorated with the outlines of giant butterflies, another in green and red. Light from the little windows gleamed from their slick surface.

We sat on the mats to eat lunch, my nose running from the burn of the chili and spices in the sambal. Tiny bananas, from a big bunch handed around the circle, completed our repast.

Afterward we gathered on the steps outside for photographs, where Tandon also interviewed Iman on video. We took our time there, sitting on the steps relaxing while Iman gave his account in Bahasa Indonesia. One little boy climbed up and sat on my lap, holding the hand of his grandmother who sat beside me. He sat patiently listening until Iman finished.

Then we thanked the Tamba family for their hospitality and returned to the white concrete road to begin our descent. Relaxed and content with our bellies full, we laughed and chatted as we slowly strolled along.

Rounding a bend between the trees on the steep upper part of the hill, we saw a group of men at the next bend. They were jumping up and down wielding big sticks and a long-handled mattock, violently beating at a pile of cut bamboo in the middle of the road. When we reached them, the men stopped beating and turned away, faces drawn, gesturing down behind them. There on the road writhed the severed tail of a cobra, with more cut sections scattered here and there. The men had beaten some parts flat, especially its head. Curious as I was, I did not crouch to inspect it too closely. The part that continued to writhe provided ample warning. The head, although beaten, might well have one last bite left. People have been killed like that, unaware that the severed heads of snakes can retain their biting reflexes for up to an hour after death. There are two types of cobra in Sumatra, the king cobra, *Ophiophagus Hannah,* and the Sumatran spitting cobra, *Naja sumatran.* Both can be deadly.

Workers must always exercise caution when cutting vegetation here, in case of snakes, but it is easy to be complacent if snake encounters are uncommon. With potentially dire consequences, and little time to react, it is no wonder everyone here was so unnerved.

Dense bamboo, such as once surrounded many of these villages for defense, would make the perfect hiding place for snakes. That so, I wonder how often snakes enter the houses, given that most buildings have no glass on the windows and have plenty of openings for ventilation.

We strolled down past big yellow lily-like blossoms, freckled with orange, which stood tall at the edge of rice fields. Then I paused. A buffalo wandered slowly across a meadow, its long grey tongue grabbing and dragging at the grasses. It was seemingly unaware of the white egret standing on its back. From uphill I heard the repetitive clay thump of mattocks. On empty terraces, between steep mud banks, men cut and turned the earth preparing for the next planting. Meanwhile other fields were already filled with standing rice.

20. Harian Boho

When we prepared to launch, two more of our party decided to join us in kayaks. Iman would paddle with us this afternoon, and Harriet. Kristin offered to accompany Harriet, who although a paddler and game for anything, had little experience.

As it would be Iman's first ever time in a kayak, I escorted him, offering him some basic tips to start. Heading out onto open water I could smell sulphur from the hot springs and fumaroles along the shores of Samosir Island. Over there I could see open scars of pale grey where rock had been quarried. This was one of the most recently active zones along the line of the caldera ring fracture, responsible for doming up the land just here. The same fracture accounts for the Pardepur domes which created Sibandang Island.

As we paddled, the sun occasionally burst through the cloud highlighting the lush green of the steep caldera slopes. It illuminated the majestic green peak of Pusuk Buhit, the sacred mountain. Some distance ahead, Saleh and Ade showed the way. There was a breeze, and there were some waves, but Iman paddled powerfully forward as if he had been a kayaker forever. But then I sensed his smile diminish a little.

"They said we were going to Harian Boho, but it looks as if they are going in here," he said. That was of no consequence. Harian Boho was not marked on my map, and one place was the same as another to me. A little later he broached the subject again.

"They are going to land here, but Harian Boho is over there in the next bay past the point."

"I'm sure it's okay," I reassured him. "They must know where we are supposed to stop for the night. Anyway, if they go the wrong way, Priyo will call them on the radio." Priyo was a little closer to shore than us and was steadfastly following the others. It appeared that everyone was on the same page. In any case, he and Saleh conversed frequently to agree details.

"But my brother and my cousin live at Harian Boho. I wanted them to see me coming in from the water in a kayak!" Now I realized his dilemma. Iman, on his first ever kayaking trip, had this one chance to arrive at his relatives' village from the water. That would be a surprise for them, and a pleasure for him. If we followed the others to our intended landing place, he would miss this unique opportunity.

"We can go and visit your family if you like," I offered. "It shouldn't take us long, and then we can paddle back." Iman was happy, and started to sing, in a rich sonorous voice, in time to his paddle strokes.

"It's a traditional Batak song," he paused to explain, "about a man who is paddling to the village where the family of his bride-to-be lives. He is excited, and a little anxious too. He hopes he will be received in a friendly way." Custom meant marriages were often arranged. The man might never have met his bride-to-be before this. He continued singing.

Then as we paddled, Iman explained what we could see. There were two bowl-shaped valleys. The valley to the left was mostly occupied by Muslims, and the valley on the right, mostly by Christians.

"Now my 70-year-old brother wants to build a big statue of Jesus, right up there on the high point of this peninsula, between the two," he explained, "and he wants to build a road all the way down to the end for a ferry landing, so tourists can get here easily. I told him it is a bad idea. I tried to persuade him to stop, but he won't listen."

At the end of the peninsula, newly turned earth marked the end of the road under construction. Then, as we rounded the corner, we could hear the rumble of machinery working high on the hillside. There was a crash and a reverberating thunder as an avalanche of rocks and dirt tumbled down the steep vegetated slope. Finally, the biggest boulders bombed heavily into the water, amid the rustle and hiss of smaller stones.

When we reached the middle of the bay, we could see a red scar that cut across the green peninsula from near the village, running all the way past the summit. Machines leveling the new road, 120 meters (four hundred feet) above the lake, were pushing aside the earth. Much of it was avalanching down the slope, crashing through the vegetation in waves. The slope was too steep for it to rest.

Reaching the Harian Boho shore we continued past the village as far as a low building, set back from the water beyond a patch of grass. At the shore, a series of concrete steps spanned the width of the property. The lowest step was under construction, with a row of white sacks of either sand or cement holding back a leveled platform of rubble, ready for concreting.

We held our position in the waves for a while, wondering whether to land or to wait until we were spotted. It would be more fun for Iman if he were seen afloat in his kayak. Happily, a man, woman, and four boys of different ages, hurried from the house to welcome him.

"You would like to come for coffee?" they asked. Iman and I looked at each other, questioning.

"The others don't know where we are, and we don't know where they went," I primed Iman.

He looked solemn for a moment and then his face brightened. "We'll phone Priyo!" he said.

That agreed, we gladly accepted their invitation for coffee, but explained that we must leave in time to find our landing before dark.

On shore, Iman tried repeatedly to call the others. He tried one number after another, but nobody answered their phone. Then, resigned to being accused of hiding ourselves, we carried our coffee out from the kitchen to a table in the breeze on the house deck. We sat beside a papaya tree that Iman's brother pointed out was not growing so well.

Now we learned that he too had kayaked, just last week, in a tandem inflatable kayak with his sister. He was so impressed by the experience he had ordered one for himself right away.

Then, changing the subject to another that seemed dear to his heart, he explained enthusiastically how he was building a road and a ferry landing to bring tourists, and money, to the village. "There will be a big statue of Christ on the hill, up there at the top."

"How long will that take?" I asked.

"It will be finished next year," he replied, confidently.

Iman said nothing, and I thought it tactful not to query whether he foresaw the project having family, political, or religious controversiality.

Behind this modern house was a traditional building. "You must come and see what we have done with it. My daughter uses it as a weaving workshop," he invited proudly.

I climbed the ladder into the wooden nest to meet his daughter, who had filled the space with her weaving equipment. It was a wonderful space for a workshop. She was busy working at a floor loom the size of a four-poster bed under a bright light, her every movement shifting shadows and shafts of light around the otherwise dark space.

Mindful of the time, we re-launched waving our goodbyes and cruised back around the point to look for the others. There we spotted our escort boat in front of a modern house at the base of the peninsula, where a large wooden boat was grounded beside a short stone dock. All the kayaks lay up on the grass above. As soon as we arrived, a chain of people helped hoist our kayaks up onto the dock and along to the grass.

Priyo promptly filled us in with the plan. We would leave our kayaks here, but tonight we would sleep somewhere else. We would drive there, up onto higher ground. But first we should move the kayaks out of the way into a covered parking space. There, they barely fit, stacked on their sides.

We threw our bags into the back of Syahrul's pickup truck and drove away, up the hill, into the dark. The roads were narrow, steep, and winding, the drop-off to the side, precipitous. Syahrul drove us carefully onward and upward into the mountains. As the night grew foggy, so his driving slowed.

When we stopped and emerged from the car, it was into a cold wind and mist. We hastened across the broad porch of a newly built house of contemporary design. Stepping through the doorway we entered the main room, as large and open as a village hall. At the near end of the room stood oversized heavy wooden tables, with high-backed benches along either side. At the far end of the room was a long serving-counter, beyond which lay the kitchen. A fire burned in a fireplace, opposite to doors leading to private rooms which we discovered were bedrooms.

Hotma Situmorang, Iman's cousin, was the owner. Emerging from the kitchen with her two young women assistants, she carried a feast, lining the serving counter with dish after dish. There were vegetables, meats, fishes both fresh and dried, eggs, sambals, and fried and steamed rice. First invited to fill our plates and eat, we were then encouraged to replenish and to sample the extra dishes that kept appearing. It was a banquet, a culinary joy.

After the hearty meal, Iman gathered everyone around him near the fire to relate the history of the Batak and of his own family.

He explained how most of his family graves were in Harian Boho, but the graves of one man and his wife were buried elsewhere. After translating parts into English, so that Harriet, Kristin, and myself could follow, he asked if it was okay for him to continue in his own tongue. It would be much quicker and easier for him, and for the others to understand. Of course, that was fine with us, but I was curious about what we had missed. The story continued late into the night, the others listening transfixed.

Finally, everyone found somewhere to sleep, some in a bedroom, but most choosing to cluster close together around the fire. Kristin and I spread our mattresses near to the door.

21. Into the Forest

Someone's phone alarm played a loud tinny jingle, at 4:30 in the morning, and continued repeating the same tune, over, and over again, for a long time. I was relieved when it finally stopped, but when I tried to get back to sleep, the alarm sounded again.

After more than thirty minutes, Kristin got up to find out whose phone it was. It must belong to one of the men lying side by side near the fire, where the sound came from, yet nobody moved to shut it off. Had they all died in the night?

It turned out to be Syahrul's, and he was still sleeping soundly. He had set his alarm to wake him in time to drive Swina into town, for her to get cash. It would take at least an hour to drive each way, so he had planned to slip away early to be back in time for our planned day. But in the event, he had overslept. Besides, Swina had not yet appeared.

Describing Batak beliefs back in 1923, Hermann Norden remarked that the Batak Institute of the University of Leyden in Holland, was collecting data about Batak adat and superstition. He relates how the Batak regard the soul as the spirit in the living body, the ghost being the spirit of the dead. The spirits of the dead would continue to exist, residing in trees, water, and rocks, revered by Batak. He elaborates:

> *But the soul may leave the body while one is yet alive;*
> *it so leaves during sleep. Therefore, it is not well to*
> *waken a sleeper for his soul may not be ready to return*
> *from the tree or rock or river where it has gone. And*

when one wakes with a headache, then it is certain that
the soul has not yet returned.

In that case, we should not have awoken Syahrul. But now, since I was wide awake, I stepped outside to greet the morning, finding it brisk and breezy, no doubt cooler on account of the clouds that occasionally fingered across the ground around me, and the extra elevation.

Shutting the door firmly from the inside against the breeze, I joined Iman at the counter, pouring myself a mug of black coffee from the flask. I felt I needed it. Then we chatted, drinking mug after mug of coffee. There was plenty of time before breakfast, which we could expect at seven-thirty. I was happy to have the opportunity to talk, for this was Iman's last morning with us. He would return home, he said, when we left for the forest.

"I go back to my wife and daughters in Jakarta," he explained. Then he grinned and turned to me. "I was forty-three when we married." He was now sixty-one, and happy.

When we drove from Tele for the Lintong forest, it was first to a part of the forest where security guards manned a checkpoint controlling access. A guard approached each car in turn. Syahrul lowered his window to speak. I did not understand what was said, but we sat with our passports ready to show, just in case. We all sat without speaking. Apparently, it is normal procedure for the guards to ask to see passports and demand a good reason before allowing any access into the plantation. But we were not there to visit the plantation. We wanted to visit the Situmorang family graves at the former village which, since the pulp company has isolated the historical heritage site, was only accessible using logging roads.

Why on earth would access be restricted? The village of Huta Sisonak lies in an area opened by Oppu Guru Sojuangon

Situmorang in 17th Century. For four hundred years, through eighteen generations, the Situmorang clan managed this forest, controlling the whole area west from Lake Toba as far as the coastal town of Barus to the south-southwest, and to South Aceh in the north. This village was sited to be central to control the region's frankincense and camphor trade, which was conducted via Barus. Cassia was also traded.

Benzoin, used like Frankincense in incense, comes from the resin of the benzoin tree, *Styrax benzoin*. According to Marsden's 1811 book, *History of Sumatra*, benzoin is extracted by slashing the bark of the trees once they reach the age of about seven years. The resin exudes from the cuts and is scraped off. The finest quality benzoin can then be harvested in the next three or four years, before the quality falls. When the tree is no longer productive, after about the age of ten to twelve years, it is cut down and the wood is split to recover pockets of poor grade benzoin.

If benzoin is obtained primarily by bleeding a tree, getting camphor is more like mining it. Camphor is extracted from the camphor laurel tree, *Cinnamomum camphora*. These trees grow wild, and if left alone can attain a great trunk girth. The circumference of the biggest trunks exceeds twenty meters (sixty-six feet). The camphor is found in crevices within the wood, but, according to Marsden, it is only found in about one tree out of ten. Unfortunately, there is no indication from the outside whether a tree will yield camphor.

To harvest the camphor, the tree is cut down and sectioned into rounds, each being split with wedges into chips to reveal the hidden pockets of resin.

Cassia was the third major commodity once traded from here. Both cassia and cinnamon come from coppiced trees of the same family and genus, and the method of harvesting is the same for each. The bark is stripped from cut branches and rolled into quills. The bark of *Cinnamomum burmannii,* which grows and is harvested in Indonesia, is reddish in color, woody, or hard, and is sold as cassia. It tastes a little spicier, or hotter, than cinnamon. Cinnamon, light brown, papery and brittle, was not grown here. It was cassia that Vera had shown us at Piltik: the long hard reddish sticks I misidentified as cinnamon.

Camphor, together with benzoin, and quills of cassia, made its way from the forest here to Barus for shipping from Sumatra's west coast, in trade for imports of iron, steel, brass wire, and salt.

Barus became such an important trading port for camphor, that camphor was widely known as *kapur Barus,* or *chalk of Barus.*

I can recall the smell of camphor from when, as a child, I suffered from whooping cough. My mother had me lean over a basin of hot water with camphor, a towel draped over my head, to inhale the warm aromatic vapor, offering some respite from my otherwise uncontrollable coughing fits.

Huta Sisonak, in the heart of forest yielding benzoin and camphor and cassia, was already long established when it became the birthplace of Oppu Babiat Situmorang, the friend and brother-in-law of King Sisingamangaraja XII. Oppu Babiat ruled over three hills and three valleys stretching all the way to the shores of Lake Toba. When King Sisingamangaraja XII was pursued by the Dutch army in Bakara, he retreated to the Lintong Forest, sheltering with Oppu Babiat at Huta Sisonak for several years. When nobody would reveal where he was hiding, the Dutch army, in retaliation, razed at least thirteen villages to the ground. Even so, no one revealed his whereabouts.

The king also had another hiding place, supposedly in a cave, hidden by a waterfall, somewhere in the Lintong area.

With two entrances, it was large enough for him to train his troops inside.

After the death of King Sisingamangaraja XII, the Dutch burned Oppu Babiat's village, Huta Sisonak, to the ground as punishment for sheltering his brother-in-law. He and his people were forcibly moved close to the lake, where they could more easily be controlled. The following year, 1908, with the collapse of active resistance against the Dutch, Oppu Babiat Situmorang signed a peace treaty with the Dutch.

Oppu Babiat was already quite old when, 16 years later, in 1924, his son Sitor was born at Harian Boho. With Sumatra still under Dutch colonial rule, Sitor, on reaching the age of six, was sent to an elementary school at Baligé. There he began his schooling in the medium of Dutch. His education then continued in Sibolga, on the coast, also under Dutch control.

The Dutch colonialists, their focus on developing resources that could be exported, cleared part of the Lintong Forest taken from the Situmorang clan. There they planted pine trees for turpentine and timber production. Then, following Indonesian independence, the new government made agreements with favored companies to take over and further exploit these plantations.

President Suharto, known by many at the time as *Mr. Ten Percent,* on account of the alleged commission he demanded on any business concessions, approved PT Inti Indorayon Utama Company. The company later changed its name to Toba Pulp Lestari (TPL) and extended the plantation territory over a wide area of what was once magnificent and diverse forest. As a result, the village of Huta Sisonak, established in the1600s, is marooned in the middle of an industrial plantation farmed by the pulp industry. It is surrounded by clear-cut, nowadays planted mostly with eucalyptus trees which are cut and replanted on a five to seven-year cycle. The trees are pulped and shipped to factories, owned by the same company but in China, where they are used in the production of rayon for textiles.

Nowadays the pulp company restricts access to the farmed area. As a concession, Hotma's family are granted special permission to visit the graves of their ancestors at Huta Sisonak, which necessitates passing through the eucalyptus farm. Hotma's husband was with us.

The plantation guard finally re-emerged from the small building and strode out in front of our car. Our reasons to enter were valid, and they would let us pass, but we must register with them again on our exit. He waved us on, his face serious below a stiff, official, uniform cap.

The logging roads wound on endlessly, rutted, potholed and bumpy, but dry. Dust flew up behind us as we shook our way past kilometers of clear-cut, with toppled stumps holding twisted fingers to the sky. We saw no animals at all, and remarkably few birds, even as we passed line after line of thin pale eucalyptus, and occasionally squadrons of pine.

Here and there, probably in ravines where planting trees would be awkward, remnants of forest stood, tall, dark, dense, and somber, but surrounded by dry cleared ground with thin pale stems. Our drive to the village would carry us for more than an hour through this landscape, which gave me plenty of time to consider the extent of this former forest, and what had happened to it.

Sumatran forests have in the past been burned and then cleared for plantations. Now, I was told, the forest is cut instead. Nevertheless, burning sometimes happens by *accident*, which speeds up the process. Once cleared, the land is sprayed with chemicals to prevent any natural regrowth before planting. I feel uneasy about that disturbing trend in the USA too, where there is an increasing use of herbicides and pesticides after clearing forest, and before planting. Clearly neither pesticide nor herbicide is good for any wild animals or plants within the actual area, but I also wonder, where do the chemicals go when rainwater drains from the land?

We drove as close as we could get to the historic village site, and then parked the cars, stepping out into the quiet of something of an oasis. Insects buzzed; butterflies danced. The air felt warm and dry.

Leaving Pak Uli and Syahrul with the vehicles, we walked down a weatherworn track into taller and denser vegetation. The sunken groove of the track must become a stream in the rainy season. When Priyo drew his *T. Kardin* parang from its sheath, with a happy smile on his face, I dropped back, out of his arms reach. The parang, a Southeast Asian knife, superficially resembles a South American machete. Heavier in the center than a machete, for chopping the woodier undergrowth here, it has a fine blade at the end for skinning, and the blade closer to the handle is optimized for carving. Priyo slashed at potential snares as he forged on, his keen blade making short work of anything blocking his way. T. Kardin, the legendary Indonesian knife maker, was one of the generous sponsors of our project, and Priyo treasured his possession.

Farther down the hill, the path became more severely rutted with potholes, scoured by rainwater, one to one and a half meters deep (four or five feet). We became increasingly hemmed in by foliage. Before we reached the village, we were reduced to bending double. Only by crouching down could we squeeze along the vague tunnel through the tangle of dense overgrown foliage: grasses, bracken, shrubs, and creepers, more than twice my height. Doubled over like this was a poor posture for good all-around vision. I could no longer effectively watch out for snakes.

Huta Sisonak, the first village of the Situmorang in this area, was well positioned on a slope close to a spring. Here I saw the bamboo hedge that Iman had primed us to look for. The dense thicket of bamboo canes, with stems as thick as birch trunks, overgrew a wall of rock and earth. This once surrounded the huta, creating an almost impenetrable boundary. We found a place where we could squeeze between the bamboo trunks.

Beyond was a spring, gushing clear, cool water. A narrow concrete stilling basin held back a head of water and allowed debris to settle out. Jetting from a spout near the top of the basin, water poured noisily into the pool below. Cemented into the step beside the basin was a stone plaque with a message. The only word I recognized was *Horas*. This was the first spring of the first village of the Situmorang of the Lintong clan.

Inside the village site stood the graves Iman described last night. There was one white painted stone sarcophagus, sheltered over by a square concrete slab of a protective roof, supported by four square pillars. The floor, over which the sarcophagus rested on a plinth, was surfaced with grey tiles.

The sarcophagus was carved and hollowed from a single piece of stone. The separate piece that formed the saddle-back ridged lid was notched along its spine. Into the front of both base and lid was carved a figure, maybe the head of a mythical singa. I saw what might have been a whorled mane, worn indistinct through weathering. Carved down the center was a long beard, or a dangling tongue. The stonework was repaired in places with cement and then painted all over white. This was the grave of the village founder, from the 17th century. I was standing in front of the resting place Sitor Situmorang described in the first verse of his tormented poem, *Pilgrimage*:

I enter the old settlement –
only the earth wall remains
with shrunken clubs of bamboo
guarding
the stone sarcophagus
half concealed by undergrowth

That sarcophagus was now at least protected beneath a roof, and the bamboo had grown back tall and dense. But all around this tiny oasis stretched the land described in that poem, where Sitor must have passed the logging concession signs and marker stakes, crossing land then newly denied to wildlife.

A simple wooden hut with a corrugated metal roof stood nearby. I stepped inside to have a look. Tools and buckets stood against the wall, including a heavy stone mortar and long handled pestle for pounding rice. There was a low metal-lined sand tray on the floor, holding the cold ash and charred remnants of partly burned wood from a fire. Above the center stood a low rack, roughly welded from rebar, to support a cooking pot above the fire.

Outside the hut and around the grave, someone had evidently cleared a patch of ground, leveling, and cutting vegetation. I imagine it could become completely overgrown quite quickly if left untended.

A short distance away stood another roofed shelter covering the carved stone sarcophagus of the founder's first son. His small conical sarcophagus was topped with the stone carving of a seated figure. This stone stopper appeared to fit loosely, with a narrow gap that Kristin peered at. It was tempting to lift the stopper to see inside, but Hotma's husband hurriedly explained something. Everyone stepped back.

Ade translated for us. It would bring bad luck to us all if anyone lifted the lid. Why? Because it would be disrespectful to the dead? No, that was not the reason, it was something else, something Ade could not explain. But it was a strong belief, or superstition, that everyone observed.

From where we stood, we could see the location of the graves of the second and third sons, down the hill and partially hidden by the undergrowth.

I tried to imagine Huta Sisonak in the days when it was surrounded by magnificent natural forest, the trees loud with bird song and the calls of monkeys and orangutans, and occasionally, yet unsettling, the deep rumbling growl of a tiger. Houses, and granaries once stood here. Below, the land leveled into terraces was likely for rice cultivation. Other plots would have yielded crops of maize, root vegetables, peppers, and water spinach. Fruits and nuts would have grown around in the forest, where building materials such as rattan, timber and palm fiber were sourced.

Camphor and frankincense from the forest around here made its way as far as the eastern Mediterranean from at least as far back as 2,000 years ago. That was long before this village was founded, so Huta Sisonak was well placed to continue this trade.

At this village, there would have been families: men, women, and children. I could imagine dogs, chickens, and pigs running loose, buffalo and maybe cattle. Women would have worked their looms outside in the alaman or sheltered under the houses. Colorful yarn, dyed using ingredients collected in the forest, would have hung to dry. Harvested rice and maize would be spread to dry in the open. There would have been the smell of woodsmoke, the sound of rice and maize being pounded, and chatter.

Nowadays, instead, there is the export of dissolving wood pulp, shipped by Toba Pulp Lestari to their sister company Sateri in China via an intermediary of their own in Singapore. Sateri creates and markets viscose rayon fabrics from managed plantations of eucalyptus. The high-grade fiber produced for 100% biodegradable fabrics, they state on their web site, depends on receiving pulp in the category of dissolving wood pulp.

To quote Sateri's sustainability commitment, from its web site:

Sateri does not source wood pulp from natural, ancient, or endangered forests.

That is true. It is sourced from trees grown in place of forest that has been eliminated. The Dutch were responsible for the first plantations of pine, the rest of the available land has been the result of clear-cutting since.

...Our dissolving pulp comes from sustainably managed plantations of eucalyptus trees, which mature in just five to seven years. This combines a steady, sustainable supply with rapid reforestation when harvested areas are replanted.

The clearcutting of natural forest continues. For example, in 2009, Toba Pulp Lestari razed an area of communal forest, to the south of here and west of Bakara, used for centuries by the villagers from Sipitu huta and Pandumaan for harvesting benzoin for a living. The logs from the clear-cut were taken for TPL profit and eucalyptus planted in their stead, removing the livelihoods of the villagers.

Of course, TPL showed authorizing paperwork from the government in Jakarta, so the villagers had little recourse. And Sateri rightly states, it does *not source wood pulp from natural, ancient, or endangered forests.* The pulp itself comes from the farmed eucalyptus planted after the ancient forest has been cut.

Ironically, Indonesia has recently shown the world that it has reduced its rate of deforestation, hopefully recognizing the value of its unique ancient forest, with its rich and diverse profusion of fauna, plants and fungi that are found nowhere else in the world. But is reducing the rate of deforestation a step toward halting it before it is forever lost?

Not necessarily. It depends on what you call a forest. If, as is the case here, monoculture eucalyptus farms are categorized as forest, then the recorded rate of deforestation on paper could drop to zero, if each newly felled block of natural forest is replaced with plantation. It is the rate of loss of natural forest which should be recorded, whatever that natural forest is replaced with.

Saleh, gazing across the landscape observed that it taken us at least an hour to drive here, adding, "You know, we are probably only thirty minutes' walk from where we stayed last night."

He might have been right, but at about five kilometers away as the crow flies (three miles), it would have been a run, and as we now knew, not all tracks were straight or easy. It was immaterial; despite being so close, we had to follow the long way around to obtain permission.

Turning our backs on Huta Sisonak, we pushed back through the overgrowth up the potholed track to find Syahrul and Pak Uli patiently waiting. Then, jostled in the pickup truck, I stared from the window at the vastness of the clear-cut. Syahrul, at the wheel, deftly negotiated the humps and bumps, streaming Creedence Clearwater Revival songs from his iPhone through the truck's stereo. It was becoming a soundtrack we were to associate, not only with Syahrul, but also with Lake Toba.

I was ready for lunch by the time we reached Hotma's house again, where the cold wind kept blowing the door open, sucking billows of smoke from the fireplace into the room. Then, while

144

everyone took the opportunity to recharge their electronic devices, I saw I had time to explore the grounds.

Opposite the spacious porch was a pond, bordered by grasses and flowering shrubs. A pathway of circular steppingstones led like lily pads toward a low, gently arched bridge. I swung open the decorative orange gates and crossed the bridge to a well-constructed open sided gazebo, with benches beneath a pyramidal roof. From here I could look out over the water in any direction, for the gazebo covered most of the island.

I was tempted to sit. It was the perfect place to linger, to contemplate the tranquility of the pond, to stare at the reflections of the blossoms of the potted shrubs. It was only the chill breeze that decided me to do otherwise. It felt noticeably cooler at this elevation, 1,800 meters (6,000 feet), than it had beside Lake Toba, nine hundred meters lower (3,000 feet).

Behind the house, a loosely fenced area, extending toward a belt of trees, was cultivated with garden crops. Clumps of tall maize were interspersed with vegetables and shrubs, some bearing pods, others unfamiliar fruit. I could see nobody at work, although someone must have invested a considerable amount of time and effort. Standing there I felt very relaxed, so much so that I wondered why the sight of garden plots should be calming. I spent a few more minutes simply staring before I heard voices behind me. It was time for us to return to the lake, to where our kayaks waited.

22. Sitor Situmorang's grave

Our way, zigzagging down the mountainside, afforded little room for complacency. Despite the narrowness of the road, vehicles sped into view around blind bends, frequently zipping by at speed, seemingly oblivious to the rough cliff on one side, and defying the precipitous drop on the other. I for one was glad that Swina had chosen our drivers, Syahrul and Pak Uli, for their conscientious driving. But there was a special place we wanted to visit on our way. Mount Pusuk Buhit was, as Sitor Situmorang wrote, the best place to go to see around. It was the volcano where King Batak chose to settle and is held sacred for that reason. Sitor wrote about it in his poem Pilgrimage, and our pilgrimage followed his.

Our route climbed the side of Pusuk Buhit, the green dome that had been so prominent in our view when we kayaked toward Harian Boho. Having appreciated the beauty of the peak from the water, we hoped to reach a high viewpoint on it from which to see the lake. But it was not to be. Low cloud misted in around us, and it rained. Unfortunately, there would be little to be seen from any higher in this weather.

We paused at an information site, Sopo Guru Tatea Bulan, at Sianjur Mulamula, where steps climbed into the downpour. Statues above here represent the descendants of King Batak, and their legendary mounts: dragons, lions, tigers, horses, and elephants. But it was at the nearby museum that we intended to spend more time, learning about the series of eruptions that created the current caldera, which has since become partly filled by Lake Toba. A video introduction, and then interactive displays in the museum, helped clarify my understanding of the series of events that led up to the cataclysmic YTT, *Youngest Toba Tuff*, eruption some 74,000 years ago.

I learned how the collapse of the steep post-eruption southeast caldera wall created the Uluan Peninsula, with its tilted block faulting. That would have happened before the precipitous caldera walls, at first cliffs, eroded away into the steep scarps seen nowadays. I learned how after this, the caldera gradually filled with water, creating the lake. The fractured lake floor was then pushed up by underlying magma into the resurgent dome that created Samosir Island, with its surface veneer of ancient lake sediments. Even more recent volcanic activity produced Sibandang Island and then Mount Pusuk Buhit.

Adjusting our plans for the weather, we descended the long winding road to the lake shores to Harian Boho, to find the grave of Sitor Situmorang and pay our respects. His grave lies close to where Iman and I stopped for coffee on our kayak detour. Sitor was born there and it was where he wanted to be laid to rest.

Without Iman for local knowledge and directions, it took us several passes in the car before we found the right place to turn aside and stop. We walked the last few paces to his grave in light rain.

Sitor Situmorang is buried, according to his own wishes, not beneath an elaborate monolith but under a simply inscribed river rock. After his death at his home in Apeldoorn, in the Netherlands in 2014, his earlier words have come true: *The lost son has come back* to Lake Toba.

Resting across the rock lay a modest wooden cross, black-painted and bearing his name. Close to his grave was another grave marker: a smaller river stone, with a simple black painted wooden cross. This one bore the name of *Tio Minar Situmorang, born Gultom*; his first wife, who died in 1996. Somber, we lingered beside the grave, misted by teardrops from the sky, some of us huddled in the shelter beneath a tree, others taking refuge beneath the eaves of the house adjacent.

I looked beyond the grave, across the rice fields, and saw a stone wall beneath a thicket of bamboo. A woman made her way on foot just outside that boundary, carrying a box on her head. I could just make out a narrow gap in the wall, presumably the gateway access through the fortification into a hidden village. Gradually, I was beginning to recognize some of the details that Iman, son of Sitor and Tio Minar, repeated so often and described so well.

Thinking of Russian nesting dolls, from little to large, I could imagine being inside the cocoon of a house, dreaming. From inside a house, in a village, within a bamboo enclosure, surrounded by fields, once maybe surrounded by forest, within the cradle of the Toba caldera, dreaming of beyond all that. Dreaming of a whole world to explore.

I could imagine in reverse, dreaming of crossing that caldera rim to see the lake, the fields, the bamboo and so on, until climbing the familiar steps to arrive home. I could also imagine those who wander far, like Sitor, dreaming to return one last time to be laid to rest.

There was another clue that a village lay hidden behind the bamboo, across the rice fields. Just outside the wall of the far village stood a three-tiered mausoleum, its upper level the saddleback shape of a house. More grandiose than Sitor's choice of a commemorative rock, but nevertheless a final resting place between the mysterious lake and the steep grassy scarp of the caldera rim. The bones of those from around the lake are often brought home to rest.

Leaving Sitor and Tio Minar, we continued along the narrow road to the almost impossibly tight hairpin turn, from the main road, into the drive that led to the lake. There, as we maneuvered carefully, a row of grey monkeys sat beside the road watching expectantly, like homeless people at a road intersection waiting for a handout. Their intention was clear enough; they had no need of a cardboard sign.

When we pulled up at the waterside house, Mrs. Julita Saragih, the Indonesian representative of the *Rudy Project*, was there to greet us. The Rudy Project, the Italian sports sunglasses company from Treviso, Veneto, sponsored us with sunglasses for this trip. Julita is not Italian but Toba Batak, something she proudly divulged upon greeting us. When Priyo first approached Rudy Project for sponsorship, he never guessed he would be connecting directly with a representative who held Lake Toba so dear. We felt honored that she had taken the time to come to meet us, and to find out how our trip was going. Since we were all already either wearing or carrying our sunglasses, we took the opportunity to pose for some promotional photographs with her.

Here we also met two local teenagers, Batak Scouts, Irvan Evendi Piliang, and Roosen Gabriel Manurung, who lived on Samosir Island. They would join us for a few days. We all pitched our tents close together, with the entrances facing the lake, and prepared to camp. The children, at least some who belonged to the family who lived in the house, were keen to interact. Curious about the tents, they peered inside to see what went into them. They also seemed to enjoy hanging out on the handrailed roof of the beached boat.

That derelict vessel I noticed when I first arrived by kayak measured about eighteen meters long (sixty feet), with an extended low roof. Pulled up steeply onto the shore, it sat proudly upright beside the dock. A gangplank crossed to its rotting deck, but the roof with its bent safety rails was still sound. Was it originally grounded for repair, restoration, or storage, I wondered? Most likely its lake days were over by the time it was hauled ashore. Whichever reason, it will likely remain here. Moss and small ferns grew from the cracks in the blistered paint. Saplings and shrubs created a stormy sea at its side. How long would it take to crumble away, once laid to rest undisturbed in a climate like this?

As the sun dropped low, woven plastic mats were unrolled onto the grass near the tents in readiness for our evening meal. Elfrida Sitohang, a young pregnant woman, and her family had cooked a sumptuous feast for us with pork, prepared in several different ways. There was also chicken satay on wooden skewers, a selection of freshly made sambals, water spinach, and of course rice. Elfrida was one of a family of ten siblings whose father was a music teacher. As we were to discover, all the siblings were keen musicians who enjoyed playing together.

Two men carried out a sheet of corrugated metal and dropped it onto the grass in front of the mat. First spreading earth on it to protect the grass underneath, they piled on wood and kindled a fire.

Cars trundled down the hill, headlights flashing in the trees. Motorcycles roared and revved, pulling up near to the house. Greetings rang out above the noise of the engines. These were Elfrida's siblings, and the whole family was clustering, welcoming and acknowledging each other in the flicker of firelight. Casually, they carried musical instruments from the vehicles to arrange, informally, a little back from the fire. We were in for a surprise live performance and the band had arrived.

One of Elfrida's brothers brought his narrow, wooden, two-stringed, boat-shaped lute, *hasapi* to play. This was acoustic, but when I examined it closely, I saw it was also fitted with a pickup for amplification, although no amplifier was needed tonight. The instrument was fretless. The body and neck, all-in-one, appeared to be carved from a single piece of wood. The thin wooden face, incorporating the upright bridge, was carved from another.

Next, there was a row of five musical drums, *taganing*, going up in size along the row to a sixth much larger drum, the *gondang*. These were mounted in a low rack at waist height, ready to be played by a seated drummer. The first drummer traditionally plays the taganing, while the second drummer plays the gondang. Each drum is tuned to a different musical note.

These drums were in the same style as those that traditionally hung on the balconies of a King's house. A thick round wooden plate at the base of each was connected by cords to the drumskin. Wooden wedges, driven between the cylindrical wooden body of the drum and the base, were used for tuning. Nowadays, the drumskins are cut from the hide of water buffalo, cow, or goat, although Iman had said that in the past, they sometimes used the skin stripped from the backs of enemies.

Playing these drums was frowned upon by the church, since the drums played such a pivotal role in the religious ceremonies conducted by the datu. By demonizing the drums and their use, the missionary directly opposed the datu, undermining his authority, and the Batak beliefs. This antagonistic approach was sure to provoke bitterness and direct conflict, unless the datu converted to Christianity. It was clear that the missionary sought to replace the datu as the conduit to higher spiritual powers. Nommensen feared for his life at Sigumpar, near Baligé, on account of the local datu.

Drums, some of the most ancient of musical instruments, have always held a power of their own. So, it seems fitting that some use of drums has persisted in Toba Batak ceremonies. Drums did survive, despite the new religion, even if some of the mystique faded. More recently they have been used in recreational, not just ceremonial music, and not only by men but also by women, even when pregnant; Elfrida was an excellent drummer.

For Batak Toba, the taganing can carry a melody, which is unusual, for drums are more typically used to mark a rhythm, keeping time. As far as I know, melody-carrying drums are only found in three regions of the world: Uganda, Myanmar, and Toba.

Available also tonight was an acoustic guitar, and a side-blown bamboo flute, *sulim*, but the guitar was not played during the first part of the evening.

Those women not playing in the band, dressed themselves in ulos and prepared to dance. Then the music began. The young children played under the feet of the dancers, who ignored or at least tolerated them, despite sometimes almost tripping. The children clearly enjoyed maneuvering their little toy construction trucks, happy to be at the center of attention, between the band and the fire.

After the family had played for some time, and we had finished eating, Elfrida encouraged the women in our group, Swina, Harriet, and Kristin, to join in the dancing. She brought out ulos for them to borrow, and the local women showed how to secure them so they would not slip off the shoulder. Having rehearsed the movements and dance steps together, the music started again, and the fun continued.

In dancing, the hands of the Batak women are very expressive. Kristin commented that the women especially, but the men too, seemed to use their hands eloquently in daily interactions, more so than in most other cultures. This dexterity

153

and relaxed hand suppleness while dancing, became even more noticeable when I watched Kristin and Harriet. Their hand movements, slightly self-conscious and almost awkward by comparison, were those from a different culture.

With the dinner plates gathered, the dancing having subsided, and the instruments set aside, the family stood chatting while jugs of tuak were passed around. It was time for the guitar to be tuned and handed from player to player. Songs and melodies drifted out across the lake into the night.

Pak Uli was especially happy. He strummed the guitar with his long fingernails and sang from the heart, a wide tooth-filled smile breaking out across his upturned face. He loved creating music, and always enjoyed drinking tuak.

I wished Iman had not left for Jakarta earlier. We missed him here. He would have enjoyed the evening.

23. To Pangururan

I heard that the village chief lived somewhere on the lower ground behind the bay. I sat in the early morning sun, scanning the land for a traditional house, perhaps more elaborate than others nearby. Seeing no prominent building, I became distracted by a small boy in a red shirt. He was struggling across a field carrying a banana leaf bigger than himself. As a child I built shelters from sticks and bracken, but it took many armfuls of bracken to roof a shelter. This boy would need little more than a single leaf to do the same. What would it be like to grow up here?

As I watched him struggle with his leaf, another little boy, Tito, approached me with his always smile, demanding our normal *high-five*. We counted out loud together: "One, two, three, four, High-Five!" and he raised his arm above and behind his head. Throwing all his weight behind it he slapped his tiny palm hard against mine, laughing! He was learning his numbers in English, and he wanted me to do it again, and again. I looked back down into the valley. The boy in the red shirt, like an ant with an impossibly big load, was still making progress.

There was one toilet, in the house beside which we camped. Since there was a large family here, plus a crowd of us, some taking time for a scoop shower, I found myself waiting in the shade outside the door to the house. Upside down on the concrete beside the door lay a large black beetle, waving its armored legs slowly and feebly. Was it a scarab?

I crouched to look more closely. It was fully five centimeters long (two inches), with fine ginger hairs under the upper legs. Otherwise, it was all over silky black, not glossy. I turned it over, surprised that neither the dogs running past, nor the young children, had so far offered it a second glance. Its wing cases were smooth, in fact all three segments were rounded and black. Slowly and deliberately, it dragged its way forward. Sometimes a leg failed to get enough traction on the smooth concrete, repeatedly scraping the surface with sharp claws.

"Have you tasted those?" Harriet's voice was at my ear. She pointed to a plate of canapé-sized treats that sat on a table near the door. They were colored variously bright leaf-green, and deep root-purple. Our hosts, standing just there, encouraged us to eat. The treats, robust enough to be finger food, trembled like jellies and were neither savory nor sweet. I guessed they were made from rice with gelatin and then colored leaf-green or root-purple, but my local language inadequacy left me speculating.

Harriet was already packing to leave us this morning, her part in our trip ending. We would miss her cheerful presence, her irrepressible positivity, and her ready chuckle. She planned to travel north to Medan, and then west to visit the reservation, Bukit Lawang, where she hoped to see orangutans. She was excited about her plans.

The orangutan is Asia's only genus of great ape, and there are three known species. While the Bornean orangutan, *P. pygmaeus*, is found only on Borneo, the other two species are found only on Sumatra. Sumatran orangutan, *Pongo abelii*, was thought to be Sumatra's only species, but in 2017 a second species was identified. This is Tapanuli orangutan, *P. tapanuliensis*.

Once widespread, and around here living freely in the Linton forest before it was felled, orangutans are in critical danger of extinction. On Sumatra, habitat loss is one of the main reasons why there are only some 14,000 Sumatran orangutans, and just eight hundred Tapanuli orangutans, left in the wild. The orangutans in the north, in the reservation where Harriet hoped to see them, are of the more numerous Sumatran species.

The day was already hot when Syahrul drove Harriet and Swina away. Swina would help Harriet find some gifts she wanted to buy, then ensure she reached her plane on time.

After Tandon finished filming and we had packed the tents, we said goodbye to the lovely family here. There was heartfelt sadness in parting, and both they, and we, expressed our hope that we would return. What they gave of themselves in preparing the meal and performing for us last night was precious and memorable. Amongst some sad faces, the little boy, *Tito with the high fives*, just kept on smiling. He was a happy boy.

Today, we were honored to have Hotma and her husband join us on the water, on their inflatable tandem kayak. Everyone aimed for Pangururan, the town in the distance. Unfortunately, making a beeline meant paddling down the center of the waterway, midway between Samosir Island and the mainland. This was against the full force of the wind. Every time someone stopped for a brief rest, or to call on the radio, everyone else stopped, and the whole group sailed rapidly backward.

Pangururan, at the bridge of land joining Samosir to the mainland, is the capital of Samosir Regency. This Regency encompasses its namesake island and extends inland to the west. From a distance we could see large buildings along the shore, spreading around the end of what appeared to be a continuous bay, but we could not make out sufficient detail for Priyo to pinpoint something to aim for. There was one prominent building, shaped like a traditional house, but immense. It made a good landmark. That was a Roman Catholic church. It stood somewhat to the right of where we needed to go, and somewhere to the right of that church, from our viewpoint, would be the town market.

Preferring to seek out a more sheltered route, Kristin and I took Irvan, one of the Toba Batak scouts, aside to the mainland intending to show him how, by skirting the shore, it would be possible to rest from time to time without being blown back. Yet when we reached shore, I was surprised how many men sat at the edge of the reed beds throwing out fishing lines. This kept us from the most sheltered water close against the shore. Despite this, and the slightly longer distance involved, our progress was faster and easier.

Although we were bound for the Tano Ponggol canal, or nearby, it was still not obvious where the entrance was. It seemed we were approaching the dead end of a wide bay. The canal must cut through the low land into the shore somewhere to the west of most of the town, but my map lacked sufficient detail.

Seeing the numerous fish farms and platforms, we decided to shortcut across the corner of the bay. We could ferry glide across the gaps and use the platforms as windbreaks to rest behind. Above us, two large birds of prey, probably eagles, swung in wide circles.

Leaving Irvan with Kristin, I paddled back to rejoin the others, skimming effortlessly with the wind pushing me along. I wanted to be sure everyone else was okay. Priyo today towed an empty yellow kayak, the result of our miscalculating how many people would paddle. We did not realize our mistake until after the escort boat started on its 100km (60 miles) circuit back around Samosir Island. It would meet us at the other end of the canal since the canal was currently under reconstruction and closed to boat traffic.

The inflatable kayak was short and floated high. The wind caught it and spun it around so much it could make little progress. Hotma and her husband found it easier to paddle powerfully when given help to keep their kayak straight.

Samosir surely originated as an island. Magma pushed up the lake floor until a dome emerged from the water. Either the continued land rise, or a fall in the water level in the lake, exposed the land bridge that joins Samosir to the mainland.

There must have been a portage route here for solus at one time, for the low neck of land from south to north is only one kilometer (less than a mile) even in the absence of creeks. But a portage was no option for large boats.

The Dutch are famed for engineering canals. In 1619, after the Dutch East India Company attacked and destroyed the city of Jayakarta on the island of Java, they dug a series of canals and built a new city exclusively for Dutch habitation around them. This city, the headquarters for the Dutch East India Company, was named Batavia. It is now called Jakarta. It turned out that the canals at Batavia were not such a smart idea. They became polluted, creating an ideal breeding ground for disease. Batavia became one of the unhealthiest places in the world.

When Captain Cook left England, in August 1768, on his groundbreaking voyage of discovery, his ship, *Endeavor*, was manned by a crew of ninety-four. Landing at Batavia on October 10th, 1770, for ship repairs, all his crew, barring those lost in the occasional accident, were in perfect health.

When he left in December of the same year, forty of his crew, stricken with malaria and dysentery, were too seriously ill to work. Seven had already died. The rest were in poor health.

A quarter of his crew died during the next two months at sea. At one point, with so many ill, only twelve men were fit enough to work the ship, and even they were in poor shape.

But a canal here, filled with the pristine waters of Lake Toba, was a different matter. With colonial control of Samosir Island, the Dutch dug the Tano Ponggol canal in 1907, the same year they killed King Sisingamangaraja XII. That was despite local hostility to the plan, opposition which Hermann Norden described in his book, *Golden Gate to Golden Sun,* in 1923. He recounts the story as told by the Dutch official he traveled with, who was on his way to help settle a water dispute, between lowland farmers and highland dwellers at Bakara.

You perhaps know the difficulty we had when the Dutch government decided to cut through the six hundred feet of land which connected Samosir with the mainland. The proposition was made, and the Batak rose in protest. It was nothing to them that our boats had to sail all the way around the huge peninsula; their prahus could be carried across. Finally, we learned the real reason for their protest. It was terror. They believed that the strip of land was the only thing which kept Samosir from sinking into the water, and so drowning the eighty thousand people who lived on it.

...At last, the Batak declared that they would never consent unless all the Dutch officials should congregate on the island while the cutting was being done. Whether they reasoned that the Dutch would not take the chance if there were danger, or whether they thought the drowning of the eighty thousand would be worthwhile if they could get rid of so many Dutch, I don't know. But the officials did congregate there; and every Batak chief was invited. It was a great occasion.

The depth of the canal was a maximum of three meters (ten feet) and frequently shallower; enough no doubt for its original purpose. Nowadays, despite dredging, it is too shallow for today's lake cruise boats and ferries. The present reconstruction, to triple the width and deepen the canal to nine meters (thirty feet) should address that, with regular dredging.

It gave me pause for thought that forty percent of all land in the Netherlands lies below sea level, with the lowest point at 6.7 meters (twenty-two feet) below mean sea level. The highest land elevation there is at 322 meters (1,058 feet). Here the canal construction is at more than nine hundred meters (nearly 3,000 feet), significantly higher than any land in Holland. So, although this shortcut is no engineering marvel, it must be one of the highest elevation canals ever dug by the Dutch, and one of the shortest.

We all converged toward the western edge of Pangururan, and regrouped there, out of the wind, at the base of a flight of stone steps that scaled the high stone bulwark. This wall buttressed a length of shore to the east of the canal, above which ran a residential road. Climbing out into shallow water, we tethered our kayaks and left them floating, under a watchful eye, while we climbed the steps to the street above.

On land, Hotma took the lead, gathering us together to explain that her sister owned a café in Pangururan.

"It is normally closed on Sundays," she clarified as we walked down the street in our paddling clothes, "but she will open it for us today." She was excited to see her sister, and to disclose how she paddled here. I could imagine that a little of that Batak pride, and competitive spirit, could go a long way to help spread an interest in kayaking all around the lake.

The waterfront street showed a different character from others we had seen. It was more European in style, and with some Dutch colonial influence. There were decorative metal fences, landscaping, and immaculate lawns. The narrow waterfront promenade running atop the seawall, afforded the best lake view.

Hotma's sister's husband, wearing a smart Navy cap with insignia, greeted us on the street. He was either still in, or retired from, a position of rank in the Navy. He encouraged us onward, until shortly we reached the refreshingly cool shade of the street corner café. There we found ourselves seats at the casual tables.

Opening our packed lunches, and about to eat, we were surprised by an unexpected treat. Hotma's sister and her staff brought us deep fried cassava cakes, fresh brewed coffee, and tiny, sweet bananas.

Suddenly I could hear a commotion in the street outside. Voices, calling over a loudspeaker, grew louder. Then a large farm or construction truck, its loading bed packed with people, slowed to a stop at the street junction by the café. It lingered there for a moment. The amplified voice, excitedly delivering some urgent message, precluded our talking. While they waited, and with our conversation paused, we watched the people crammed in the back of the open truck. They waved and shouted but then leaned out at us and cheered, waving more vigorously on seeing us inside the café.

The truck then turned the corner and accelerated away, followed closely by police cars and more trucks in procession. As each vehicle stopped outside the café before turning, everybody on board had time to spot us strangers, and to shout and wave at us. When it was calm enough for us to talk again, Saleh explained there were local elections coming up. The candidates were campaigning.

The coffee tasted good. Tandon bought several bags of different types to sample later. "We'll try some for breakfast tomorrow when we are camping," he offered, generously.

24. Dutch Canal

Our appetites comfortably satiated, we left Hotma and her husband with her sister, and launching again, towed the spare kayak into the canal. Here it was noisy, dusty, and smoky. Heavy earth-moving machines were cutting the canal wider, building the banks up with earth and smoothing the incline.

Where the banks had been smoothed, teams of workers spread big white sheets of fabric across, pinning the sheets down. A portable crane hoisted large concrete slabs, one by one, from a mold on the bank. Guided by the team on foot below, the crane lowered each slab into position to surface the canal bank. The already completed section was a smooth, steep, uniform slope of pale grey, a perfect canal embankment.

The canal grew shallow, clogged with waterlogged vegetation, narrowing ahead between overgrown banks. Stone walls bulwarked the upper banks, supporting the only bridge that connects Samosir to the mainland. This low narrow bridge, twenty-five meters long (eighty feet), with its yellow-painted concrete posts and red tubular guardrails, today spanned a virtual gap. It looked down onto mounds of overgrown earth, which filled the canal from bank to bank and blocked our way. Presumably, this was part of the construction plan.

A longer bridge reaching three hundred meters long (330 yards) is scheduled to replace this one, whereupon this infilled section will be re-opened and widened.

An early photograph, from shortly after the completion of the canal in the early 1900s, shows a low footbridge, with a section raised to allow two small boats to pass. A crowd of people watch from both banks, waiting for the bridge to drop again so they can cross.

The new road bridge will reach eight to nine meters (25-30 feet) above the canal. It will accommodate two lanes of traffic on the street, while the larger lake tourist cruise boats will be able to pass underneath.

We reached the end of the channel at the bridge, and I feared a long, tough, portage ahead. Saleh clambered up with Ade to scout the way, and one by one we followed, lifting the kayaks awkwardly up the treacherous muddy bank. The narrow paths that pushed through the lines of least resistance around and over hummocks, twisted through knee-high thickets of thorny undergrowth and blade-edged leaves. It was awkward to portage without snagging the kayaks and tearing our skin. But from the high point under the bridge, I saw our way forward: a stretch of muddy ochre-yellow water, but then another barrier.

Launching through mud, we almost immediately reached the second barrier to find just a narrow connecting channel, with the opaque colorful water slowly bleeding, like paint, into clearer water on the other side. It was just wide enough to float a kayak through, but not deep enough without getting out first.

A plank spanned the gap as a footbridge, over which the first two kayaks were lifted. Then, at Kristin's suggestion the plank and some boulders were moved aside, so we could float the other empty kayaks through. Finally, it seemed, we were free to go.

The water here was reasonably clean, so we assumed we had rejoined the lake, but in truth there was one more blockage to come. Construction workers were building a new causeway, across which they were driving trucks to dump dirt and debris to make the crossing more substantial. All this was to construct a temporary crossing for the trucks and machinery working on the canal, which would otherwise repeatedly cross the narrow bridge. It was noisy, with trucks already lined up, waiting their turn to dump their load, and not leaving enough time for us to cross.

We waited. Finally, workmen came to see what we were doing. They held up the traffic for just long enough for us to scurry across with our kayaks and launch on the other side.

There, we paddled out to an uninterrupted view of the volcano, Pusuk Buhit. The summit stood 4.3km away (less than three miles) to our left, at more than a thousand meters elevation above the lake (more than 3,500 feet).

This was the area of Lake Toba inhabited by the first Batak, King Batak. He is thought to have come from the coast, probably from Barus, settling at the foot of Pusuk Buhit at a place called Sianjur Mulamula. The area encompasses most of the land around the mountain, all the way along the mainland shore from Harian Boho past where we now sat.

All the Batak tribes descend from the children of his two wives. One of those family lines became established at Bakara and led to the Kings Sisingamangaraja I-XII. Batak men, we understood, must learn, and remember their hereditary line, going back through the generations to the starting point of King Batak, here, some eight-hundred years ago, and adhere to the adats that define such matters as which families a man or woman may marry into, and which they may not.

Our support boat met us in the bay to the north of the canal, where Saleh and Ade, who were to attend a meeting on the mainland, lifted their kayaks on board. The boat also carried the extra kayak Priyo had towed. As I sat waiting, I took in the scenery. Pusuk Buhit stood behind, largely unforested, and with a pale grey scar down the slope toward the lake. From here the scar looked like a quarry, or a landslip, with buildings clustered at its base, but this was hot, volcanically active, open ground with solfataras: disintegrated volcanic rock with vents leaking sulfurous gases and steam. There are hot springs too, and some of the buildings are spas.

By the time the boat left, we were a compact team of five. Only Irvan and Roosen remained with Kristin, Priyo and me.

On this side of the island, the water was shallow, and we could see the bottom, with the weed growing up from it. It felt different from the steep, deep, outer shores of the caldera.

Pangururan was, and still is, a market town. At the start of the 20th Century, and presumably from long before that, the market was held here, on the north side of the canal, not actually in the town of Pangururan. Its location, just a kilometer, (1,000 yards) from where the canal emerges at its northern end, would have always been convenient for people from both the mainland around Pusuk Buhit, and from Samosir Island.

With the cutting of the canal, the location became even more convenient for anyone coming from the south. A Solu bolon could easily pass through the canal to beach here and unload its cargo, in full view of Pusuk Buhit.

To the north, on the opposite side of the lake some twenty-seven kilometers (18 miles) away on the mainland shore, is Haranggaol, another market town. That market is well positioned to receive trade goods coming up the river route from the east coast of Sumatra, via Medan.

I can imagine solus arriving at Pangururan market from Haranggaol carrying goods from the east coast, and Malaysia and beyond, while other goods were brought in via Sumatra's west coast and carried overland from Barus.

In the early 1900s, livestock markets here sold goats, cattle, and horses on different days. At that time, dog meat was also in high demand at the general market here, and in other local markets. Hermann Norden describes a market at Tarutung in 1923:

> *Pasar (Market) day is a social occasion. But when I found a large group assembled in one place, I discovered it was that most interesting, because most gruesome, spot in a native Pasar - the dog market. Now dog meat is a delicacy among the Bataks, and more to be desired than the flesh of any other animal. Therefore, to prove that no fraud was being done, each vendor held above his display the head of the dog that had been slaughtered.*

His photograph shows about twenty men sitting on the ground on a grassy slope above rice fields. A small mat was spread in front of each seller displaying meat, presumably each display from a single dog. Every one of those seated vendors held up the head of a dog for the camera, while other men stood around behind watching.

On market days at Pangururan market, hundreds of people would have milled around buying and selling goods. Pottery, matches, pins and needles, and woven fabric would have been arrayed on the ground or on mats. The women, for the men generally only sold meat, squatted behind their wares, talking, drinking tea, and tending their babies, bartering with potential customers who made their way past.

Now there is nothing visible to suggest such a history. Most of the land bordering the beach where the market was held is cultivated in small plots. Pangururan market has moved. Nowadays it is held indoors, in a part of town beyond the southern canal entrance, on the far side of where we stopped for lunch. The site is south of the big Catholic church that was so prominent from the water. Today, about half the market area is devoted to livestock.

Paddling past the old market site we saw many more solus, both on the beach and close offshore, than we had on the steeper outer lake shore. Most on the water were wooden dugouts, with men fishing with nets.

I stopped to watch one solu. The fisherman, having hung out his net in the shallow water beneath bottle floats, circled it, maneuvering with his paddle in one hand while stabbing at the water weeds with a bamboo spear in the other. Poking at the weeds was one way to startle the fish. I saw other fishermen slap the water all around a net with a bamboo, and still others using a stick, with a weight on the end as a plunger, to make explosive splashes to scare the fish into the nets.

Once the fisherman had circled his net, he lifted it from one end and gently pulled himself sideways over the whole length, dropping any fish that were caught into a bucket as he progressed. It was a methodical and repetitive motion, pulling up the next length of net with one hand, while releasing the empty section from the other.

Water buffalo, often a female with a calf tethered to it, floated like hippos near the shore. They were inconspicuous like this. If we spotted them too late, startling both them and us, or approached too closely, they stumbled ponderously from the water.

The solus that were pulled up on the shore here resembled basking seals, the grey sheen of the wood gleaming like fur, and the head and tail ends arched up.

Children played and splashed in the water. A few men stood in the water and cleaned themselves. Later, groups of women gathered at the shore to bathe, to clean dishes or to wash clothes.

There were houses, mostly set back from the shore and partly hidden by trees and brush. There were also resorts, one with a semicircle of large saddleback red-roofed buildings all facing inward.

It was growing late when we stopped to greet a man vigorously paddling a dugout solu in the opposite direction to us. He said he was in a hurry to get home before dark, and he waved his hand in the air, looking up and all around, drawing our attention to the sky. It was dimming, but not dark yet.

He may have been in a hurry, but he was curious about our kayaks. Stopped, he took the opportunity to smoke the lit cigarette he held in his hand while he paddled. As he took long slow drags on it, the distinctive scent of cloves wafted across the water.

Smoking, especially the clove-scented kretek, is said to have become ingrained in Indonesian culture ever since the Dutch established tobacco plantations in the 1800s. Indonesia, one of the world's biggest tobacco producers, has one of the highest percentages of smokers to non-smokers in the world.

Kretek has high concentrations of tar and nicotine, up to four times that found in many other popular cigarette brands. In addition, the clove oil is harmful to the lungs. Consequently, more than 200,000 people per year here develop related cancers. Seemingly that is not newsworthy, although when that same number of people, 200,000, were estimated lost in Sumatra during the devastating 2004 tsunami, the event hit the headlines worldwide.

Undeterred, tobacco companies here still target children as their future market, guaranteeing that those cancer rates will continue into future generations. We often saw both children and adolescents smoking.

His kretek finished, the fisherman sped on his way, the pleasant fragrance of cloves still lingering.

Now threatened by darkness, we landed on a narrow gravelly shore to find our headlamps. We dug out our jackets too, since it was growing cooler, but we hurried to avoid the sandflies which swarmed from the grass. I wasted no time retreating a few yards offshore until we were all ready.

As darkness shut in around us, the sky opened to a dense powder of stars that coated the sky and swarmed in reflections beneath us. Here and there were familiar constellations. Arcing across the heavens was the bright band of the milky way. Suddenly the brilliant trail of a shooting star blazed across the sky. The sky seemed a more tangible part of the scenery, partly because so much else had faded into darkness. The stars seemed peculiarly bright away from artificial lights, perhaps clearer beneath the slightly thinner atmosphere.

From now on, the shadowy shapes of kayaks were for the large part invisible. Only the red glow of the headlamps revealed where the other paddlers were, and that glow was not always visible. Sometimes we ran into one another. Occasionally there was a crash as someone's kayak or paddle hit a pole or post planted in the shallows.

Leading the way, with my red light behind my head so the others could see it, I slammed full speed into a low fishing platform and was instantly stopped.

A fish, scared by the approach of our parallel kayaks, leaped from the water, and hit one of the boys in the face. Our laughter and roughly translated comments flew back and forth in the dark in disjointed fragments. With no comprehensible dialogue, and unable to see what was going on, I often had little idea of what was happening.

The shore here was lined with reedbeds, an easy edge to follow in the dark, although the shallows held occasional rocks which encouraged us to detour farther from shore. Priyo and the boys stopped frequently and abruptly, without warning, rapidly vanishing as they fell behind. Each time they stopped, they found our location on a cellphone using Google Maps, and then radioed it to Tandon. Meanwhile I drifted with Kristin, gazing up at the stars. We were heading for the northernmost tip of the island.

"One and a half kilometers more", Priyo announced confidently, when he caught up, his red headlamp finding my face and dazzling. Yet twenty minutes later, after checking again, he announced once more: "One and a half kilometers to go."

So, it became a joke. "How far to go now? One and a half kilometers?" Finally, we spotted a bright light swinging from side to side on the shore. We aimed for it, and there were Tandon and Ally, happy that we had finally arrived. Even in those last moments we teased Priyo that, with just one and a half kilometers yet to go, it should not take us too long now.

Tandon and Ally had waited on the sandy shore, bundled up in warm jackets against the chill, a chill which made us hasten to unload our kayaks. Leaning the kayaks against one another alongside a low wall, we followed Ally across the sand between trees. This, she said, was the campground, something that was difficult to discern in the dark.

I envied Tandon the warmth of his jacket, so the moment we reached a small covered wooden platform, by a cluster of tents, our camp having already been kindly set up for us by Tandon and Ally, I hastened to change into warmer clothes. We did not linger. It was just a short way to the camp restaurant-café.

We found it still open, although there were only two or three people there. We ordered food and beer, and I ate my meal with Guinness, while the others chose Bintang.

Bintang means *star*. A lager, it tastes like Heineken, which is not surprising since Dutch beers came into Indonesia with colonization. Bintang is an Indonesian subsidiary of Heineken, taking its name from the red Heineken star, displayed prominently on the Bintang packaging. It was late before I tumbled into the red *Eiger* tent, with Kristin, to sleep.

25. Huta Bolon Simanindo

I felt a chill in the morning air when I unfolded myself from the tent. Tandon was already up, crouched by his own tent brewing coffee. He looked content. Like me, he is fond of his morning brew and takes it strong. Cozily bundled in his down jacket, it was clear he took to camping like a lizard to a warm rock.

There was little urgency. First, our tents must dry, and for now they were in shade. The beads of moisture would not evaporate beneath my lazy gaze, but as soon as the sun hit, the tent would become ferociously hot inside. To be ready before that happened, we emptied everything into the shelter alongside. There, everything seemed to explode into chaos. All that stowed neatly into our kayaks, taking up little space, here sprawled into a jumble of drybags, sleeping mats and paddles, journals, coffee mugs and clothes. To organize, we tied some lines under the eaves of the little shelter to hang our paddling clothes, which at least separated the damp from the dry.

Cradling a coffee in my hands, I meandered slowly around the sandy campground between well-spaced trees, some with benches in their shade. Here and there were palms, and flowering shrubs, but no other tents. Colorful umbrellas and bright honeycomb balls hung above an avenue bordered with flowering shrubs. At the far end stood a large powerful sculpture of a black horse with its head bowed. As I approached, I realized it was constructed from rubber tires.

I could imagine a bustling beach scene here on a hot day. Parents would take advantage of the waterfront wooden loungers all along the shore, shading beneath the large blue and white umbrellas, watching their children run and splash. Was this the wrong season, or the wrong time of day? Did many people camp here, or was this mostly a waterfront playground? This morning the lake was quiet, whispering at the shore while loudspeakers, hidden up in the trees, played lively Indonesian pop music, setting the mood for a fun time, even before the guests had arrived.

The only activity this lazy morning was a group of workmen hand-raking the sand, and a team of several men building a wall, carrying sand from the beach to mix cement. For a moment I worried how the salt in the sand would affect the strength of the cement, but in a flash realized my unease was unfounded. This was not the sea but a freshwater lake. I am more often on seashores. Both sand and water from this lake would be fine for cement. But where did the sand come from? Was the shore naturally this sandy, yet elsewhere overgrown, or was this imported for the campground? Perhaps it came from the bottom of the lake, uplifted when the resurgent dome pushed up Samosir Island.

It did not surprise me that we were late onto the water. I launched with Kristin. Waiting, daydreaming, and drifting, I turned to see with surprise that she had scrambled up from her kayak onto one of several giant swings, each suspended above the water. With her drifting kayak tethered by her towline, she was standing, swinging herself widely back and forth above the water, higher and higher.

Her swing was suspended from a frame of four thick bamboo poles nine meters long (thirty feet), tied together at the top into a pyramid.

When Ally launched, I gave her a short lesson on how to paddle forward, and how to use a stern rudder to steer. Not having paddled before, she picked up the basics quickly enough to join us on the first part of the day. She managed her kayak well.

We reached Simanindo Complex, our first destination, less than three kilometers (two miles) east and a little south from the campground. There on the narrow shoreline of sand we lifted our kayaks onto sharp grass. I did not delay. A pin-stab on my leg alerted me to the sandflies gathering on my skin. Jumping and swatting only roused more from the infested grass. I secured my gear and hurried up the field.

Huta Bolon Simanindo is an old huta, now a museum, in the village of Simanindo. Artifacts are housed in an original traditional building, *bolon*, outside the village defensive walls.

We were led there by the owner of the homestay and museum, Tiolina Sinambela, a vivacious and charismatic woman. On display were many objects from the village: the datu staffs, the containers for potions, musical instruments, and carvings. I was most eager to see the King's canoe, the *solu bolon* about which I had heard. But I had come too late.

Tiolina led me to where it once sheltered under a roof for protection, her face a picture of regret. The roof had collapsed, she said, crushing the canoe. All that was left were some long planks and some of the internal structure. She showed me a photograph of it in its previous condition, when it was a magnificent boat, maybe 15 to 18 meters long (50 or 60 feet).

In the photograph I could see how carvings, in the same style as decorated the sides and façades of the houses, adorned the bow, stern and gunwales. The same symbolic white, red, and black paint colored the carvings.

I noticed it carried a mast with what appeared to be fabric wrapped around it: a sail or maybe a banner. Traditionally such large canoes, made from hollowed logs, carried trade goods to market. When necessary they could carry up to fifty paddlers. Although common, it must have been a dramatic sight when several of these substantial vessels converged toward the beach on a market day. There, groups of dozens of them might gather to bring or carry away goods.

Nowadays, as Tiolina told me, there were no trees left around here big enough to build these canoes. It would be prohibitively expensive to make any kind of reproduction to replace it. She looked at the wreck of hers with sadness.

Alongside the house was a short single-seater solu, dug out from a smaller log. This was the same pattern of canoe as the large ones, but the small ones were used for fishing, not trade.

We walked from there, past the graves of the ancestors. She pointed out the grave of her husband in the row behind. "When did you lose your husband?" asked Kristin. When Tiolina replied, with pain in her eyes, "Two years ago," Kristin held her hands and sympathized.

"It must be so hard for you," she said. "You must miss him very much. But you can be strong. You can carry on his memory with your work here. You have this wonderful museum and guest house to look after, and to remind you." Tiolina was clearly still mourning his loss and appreciated her concern.

The main village, *huta*, was hidden by a dense hedge of bamboo. To reach it, we passed under a stone arched gateway, through a short stone tunnel. We found ourselves at the end of the alaman, looking between a row of traditional houses, *rumah bolon*, on our left, and a row of storehouses, *sopo*, to our right.

In the middle stood an ornately carved staff, and farther along a slaughter post, *borotan*, the structure symbolizing a tree, with the customary addition of leaf-covered branches.

This was the Simanindo village, home of the Sidauruk clan. The King's house, that of Raja Sidauruk, was central on the east side. It was the former home of Rajah Simalungun, a Batak king who had fourteen wives. The roof was once decorated with the horns from ten buffalo, representing ten generations of the dynasty.

Tiolina took pleasure in guiding us around the compound. Part of the foundation of the values of Batak culture, she explained, stands on the principle of *dalihan-na-tolu*. That is like a three-legged cauldron. One leg embraces kinship within the clan. The second embraces kinship with the clans that daughters are given to in marriage. The third respects the clans that give brides to the men of the clan, the *hula-hula*. To complete the circle, each clan in the trio always offers daughters as brides to the same one of the clans, taking daughters for their sons to marry from the other. This creates a strong family bond between all three clans.

Along the west side of the alaman stood the storehouses, *sopo*, or granaries, smaller than the houses, or *rumah,* standing opposite. I took time to study a sopo more closely, remembering details from Baligé. Each was an open platform supported by the framework of wooden posts and horizontal planks, like the houses. Above the platform, the roof, under which grain would be stored, was thatched here with palm fiber, and with a saddleback roof ridge. It was supported by six stout columns as was customary. But now I spotted an additional detail I had missed before. Each column was capped by a large carved disc, or round of timber, overhanging the column to prevent rats from accessing the grain above.

We climbed to the open platform of a sopo to see a long and squared log there, with seven depressions along its length. Each bowl-shaped depression was a mortar used for pounding rice, to remove the husks by thumping down with heavy posts. This was typically a job for the women, who would stand in line, beating a rhythm as they worked. The courtyard below would have been used for drying rice.

Kristin asked if the people sang while they pounded the rice. "No," she replied, "the rhythm was enough. But I can sing."

She straightened her shoulders and sang the same song for us that Iman sang as he paddled with me toward Harian Boho, or at least one with a similar theme and melody. It was that of a man heading towards the family home of his bride to be. Tiolina's voice was beautiful and powerful: her rendition very moving.

A protective wall and a bank surmounted by a tall bamboo hedge once enclosed this whole village. Bamboo had recently been removed from one side of this rectangle leaving just the rampart, several feet tall, beyond which we could see the land slope down to the lake. The homestay stood in that direction, and the store selling ulos and souvenirs. There too was Ruma Kaca.

Ruma Kaca, or *Glass House*, was the old Dutch colonial style building where Tiolina lived. She welcomed us into her light-filled home, the sunlight streaming through sizable glass windows. It was a cozy home with piano, couches and chairs and comfortable bedrooms. It was richly decorated with souvenirs from around the world, and books and musical instruments.

On a small round table sat a huge book about textiles by the researcher Sandra Niessen, *Legacy in Cloth: Batak Textiles of Indonesia*. This lavishly illustrated tome is the definitive resource for anyone interested in the Batak woven heritage.

On the wall hung a painting in Dutch style, a nod to the architectural style of the Ruma Kaca, along with the basketful of plastic tulips. A family portrait, and many individual portraits hung on the wall too, along with a carved and painted wooden mask. Beside the piano stood an electric guitar and amplifier belonging to Tiolina's late husband. The heat and humidity had corroded the metal parts, pitting the guitar pickup covers.

It is a harsh climate for any guitar, acoustic or electric, but Indonesia is a well-known source for wood for guitar-making. Meranti is one Indonesian wood commonly used for electric guitar bodies, being easy to work, and stable, not inclined to twist or warp. It is also relatively lightweight for a hardwood. Lightweight means that it is easy on the shoulder when playing, but it typically lacks some of the brightness of sound, complexity and sustain of a heavier hardwood.

Tiolina sat and played piano, and sang for us, leaving us free to wander and look at her collections. Then we walked together to lunch in the gazebo, via the gift shop, where we were eager to peruse the handwoven ulos that were for sale.

Nearby, a big fire was rapidly consuming a mound of cleared bamboo, but I noticed that not even smoke deterred the sand flies. While eating, we made small talk and got to know a little bit more about Irvan and Roosen who were paddling with us. As it turned out, Roosen performed the traditional dances like those we had watched at Baligé. He had performed here at Simanindo.

Launching again into the gentle shallows, we paddled the few hundred meters to a narrow island, just four hundred meters long, that parallels the shore. Uninhabited, Toba Island, *Pulau Toba*, is left as a nature reserve. It is the closer of two islands. The more distant, just eight hundred meters offshore (a half mile) is Pulau Malau, named for the local clan who claimed ownership. During Dutch colonial rule, this island became a tourist destination, and was known as Tao Island, or Pulau Tao. Nowadays there is only a restaurant there.

Stopped in the shadow of the island cliff, we drifted with the escort boat to eat cookies, handed down to us, before continuing.

Before long, Tandon and Ally transferred to the boat, which would go ahead to collect Ade and Saleh from the far side of the lake. We would next see them all at the end of the day. In the meantime, we continued as our smaller group of the two boys, who were paddling strongly, Priyo, Kristin and me.

As evening approached, people congregated on the shore to bathe, and fishermen in solus pulled fish from their nets. Individuals strolled along the shore, as if walking dogs, but each leading a water buffalo on a rope. One meandered slowly, letting his buffalo graze as it went. Another stood with his feet in the water staring out across the lake, while his buffalo waded in and wallowed, cooling itself in the water. Yet another had tethered her buffalo to graze while she stood talking.

In Sumatra, in 2008, there were an estimated 1.1 million buffalo. Most were swamp buffalo, not dairy type, used for agricultural tasks instead of tractors. They are ideal in small fields and muddy conditions. They are also slaughtered for meat and used in traditional ceremonies. Water buffalo are only found in North Sumatra, where they number fewer than one thousand in total. Water buffalo are suitable for dairy, besides the other tasks. Piltik Coffee latte was creamy with water buffalo milk.

Here and there along the shore, solus were pulled up just clear of the water. On land, all appeared calm, unhurried, and serene. In contrast the lake was choppy. Waves steepened, racing across the shallows, or reflecting from steep banks into deeper water, crisscrossing and splashing as they met.

Since darkness always fell quite abruptly, it could catch us by surprise. We paused to ready our headlamps, seemingly long before they would be needed. Yet it was only a short time before we switched them on. Although we always selected red light, to see each other without destroying our night vision, other white lights around could make that pointless.

There was a bright beacon far ahead: the cluster of white lights glared from the row of buildings lining the shore where the Tuk Tuk peninsula jutted out. That was our goal. Glancing all around me, I could see a glowering rim of cloud encircling the Lake above the steep caldera slope. The afterglow of daylight still lingered high in the sky overhead, gilding a few puffs of high cloud, above the lake. On Samosir Island the shadow of cliff soared behind the low coastal strip.

Individual spots of light appeared along the cauldron rim, each reflecting from the water. Stars showed, although the new moon was not yet visible. We passed more buildings, some just square shadows on the shore and others brightly lit. I became aware how they became more densely clustered as we progressed. Gradually the shore turned into a wall of adjacent coastal developments. The closer we approached Tuk Tuk, the fancier the buildings appeared to be. Although only two storeys high, they were overlooked from behind by others up the slope, conveying an overall impression of taller buildings.

We could hear live music played loud, but we could see almost no sign of people. Was it too breezy to be out? Only occasionally did we pass a couple dining outside, or a cluster of people sitting together overlooking the water. Sometimes we heard voices wailing together over a strummed guitar.

Music seemed to be ubiquitous around Lake Toba. Plenty of people played an instrument or were happy to sing. When we could not hear live music, there was often a radio playing, or music blasting from a boat, or a café. Men and women working in the fields also often worked to the sound of music. Out on the water, where even quiet sounds carry far, with so many sources, we were rarely without a background soundtrack.

In the dark, the steep walls beneath the buildings reflected the waves as chaotic rebounds, which made our kayaks buck and twist. In one area, light streamed horizontally, low to the water. It hit the waves in such a way that it became impossible to see what was going on. Scarcely able to discern the surface, in the apparent absence of water, I was jostled by dancing pillows of light and shadow.

I caught a wave and sped effortlessly through a gap between Samosir and a rocky islet, under the strange lighting from shore. Suddenly my kayak hit something underneath and bounced. Startled it was so shallow, I slowed down, but it was impossible for me to predict the depth ahead. Had I hit the top of a rock in deeper water? Or was it generally shallower than I thought?

Tuk Tuk peninsula, shaped like a slice of mushroom with its cap in the lake, was formed when lava domes erupted along the fracture line that allowed the trapdoor uplift of Samosir. The shape would offer a natural sheltered landing somewhere, no matter from which direction the wind blew. It might seem the obvious destination for ferries from Parapat, from the east side of the lake, but car ferries instead go to Tomok, two kilometers away (a mile) to the south. Passenger ferries, however, make several stops to drop passengers, including at Tuk Tuk.

It was not until we rounded the hook of the mushroom cap on the south side that we ran onto calm water, stilling the reflections of both waves and lights from shore.

Finally, we crossed the bay, pausing in the face of a ferry which, blaring loud music, began maneuvering unpredictably. It seems that, whether on the water or on the roads, being around traffic can be a little harrowing. The ferry reversed and turned and pushed forward and turned again, drawing donuts in the bay. I was not sure where to go to be out of its way, for it accelerated swiftly each time, but just as abruptly turned and reversed. Was this an aspiring boatman eager to explore how quickly the almost empty boat could turn? Had he been drinking? Maybe it was just a display of joy, the water-bound expression of a skip in the step by the helmsman, glad to have finished for the day.

It was then we saw Tandon's light, swinging to attract us. We approached cautiously toward a seawall, and a dock of sorts. "It's a little bit awkward," his disembodied voice called out, "so come in gently." It was tricky in the dark. To disembark onto the walkway required an awkward stretch across the cushion of water hyacinth that rebuffed any close approach, and by a low netting fence that defended the edge of the path. I struggled to clamber up without losing contact with my floating kayak, and then to lift it up and over the netting. After a stimulating day, I for one felt tired and chilled.

With the kayaks emptied and stacked, we followed the path to the homestay. This place was a bewildering labyrinth. An open sided restaurant, or lounge, furnished with dining tables and armchairs and couches and low coffee tables, led to a library room and gardens. At different levels were another meeting room, or dining area, and kitchens, and some accommodations. This informal and open homestay, or guest house, was owned by a German woman and her Indonesian husband who offered an inexpensive place to stay for guests willing to help with the chores.

Most of the accommodation seemed to be nearby in a series of little apartments, tucked, like hobbit dwellings, between the overhanging trees and shrubs along the winding paths. Swina proudly showed us to the little building she had chosen for us. "I hope you like it?" she questioned anxiously. "You have it for yourselves."

From the living room, a few steps led down to a bathroom. A ladder led up to a sleeping loft. In the past, Toba Batak slept in communal spaces. That was how we too often slept as we traveled. Nowadays, the traditional houses are more likely to be inhabited by a single-family unit rather than by an extended family. To offer more privacy for parents and children, additional bedrooms are built beside or behind a house, or the original communal space is subdivided. A separate kitchen and bathroom are also usually added behind the main building.

In our private sleeping loft, at the top of a ladder under a low roof, we had a big mattress on the floor underneath the pink cloud of a mosquito net. There were mosquitoes here.

Having settled in, we followed the sound of live music to the lounge, and our takeaway meal. Saleh and Ade rejoined us there, the boat having collected them after their meeting at the far side of the lake, but Irvan and Roosen had gone home.

There were three guitars available to guests, one disabled with broken tuning keys. Of the two remaining, one was in the hands of the man we had heard from our room singing enthusiastically and loudly. He appeared to have imbibed a lot of tuak. His songs were known to the locals, who joined in. Pak Uli picked up the other playable guitar and sat down opposite to accompany, both strumming and singing along. His face beamed with a big, bright, toothy smile.

Later, when the drunken man mumbled and stumbled away, a succession of others took turns with the vacant guitar. I discovered that many of the men, if not most, could play guitar. Nobody was shy to sing along with the songs either.

We sat sipping beers, passing the guitars around, until some other guests materialized in the shadows. This group of European tourists, standing together for solidarity, asked us to quieten down. They planned an early start next morning and our singing was disturbing their sleep.

26. Ambarita Siallagan Village

Lush tropical vegetation greened our view where we met for coffee, and then shared a fresh fruit platter with our omelet breakfasts, by the garden. We were still there when Mr. Omri Samosir arrived with a few of his associates. Mr. Omri Samosir, casually stylish in gleaming new Nike shoes, smartly creased trousers, and a soft, collared, button-down t-shirt, lounged comfortably in his seat. He is the 15th generation village chief from Onanrunggu, on the south end of Samosir Island where we would stay next.

Mr. Omri Samosir had invited us to sleep in his personal family's house, almost two hundred years old. I had looked forward to visiting this special King's house ever since Saleh described it to us at the start of our trip. Mr. Omri Samosir was one of Priyo's father's friends, when they were all students together at the Institut Teknologi Bandung. He said he welcomed us to stay because he approved of what we were doing, and he trusted we would be respectful to the historic property in his care. For us, it would be a unique opportunity to sleep in a real *Rumah-bolon*, traditional home. This was the building Ade anticipated being spooky.

Mr. Omri Samosir, on the other hand, did not seem the sort of man to harbor ghosts. As CEO of a division of the huge mining company that was Inco, but is now the global mining company VALE, he worked at Lake Matano, a large tectonic lake on Sulawesi.

Relaxing comfortably now at the table, legs outstretched, he was clearly the dominant individual in today's discussions, whether he spoke or not. As Saleh and Priyo discussed our route and pointed to details on the map spread out on the table, I attempted to follow their conversational thread, which was in Bahasa Indonesia.

One part of the discussion, about paddling, was conducted in English for my benefit. I expressed my interest in the paddling culture, and how I had seen so many of the traditional solus being used for fishing. I also expressed my curiosity about how they were built. Mr. Omri Samosir said that his neighbor, just along the beach from where he lived, was a solu craftsman. He would try to arrange for us to meet him, to see how they were carved.

Finally, we all gathered under the trees for a group photograph, before Mr. Omri Samosir and his associates continued their way.

We planned to spend this whole day on land, since there was too much to be seen here to fit into a kayaking day. Backtracking yesterday's paddling route, overland by car, we hurried to reach Tiolina Sinambela at the Simanindo complex, arriving just in time for the start of a scheduled dance ceremony.

The dancers filed into the square dressed in their colorful regalia, leading a water buffalo. The minstrels up in the balcony of the King's House began to play. At the head of the procession, the buffalo was led up to and all around the slaughter post, and then tethered, its forehead against the post. There, he stood quietly, with his head in the shade: the leafy branches refreshed since we were here yesterday. Now the first prayer was conducted, a prayer that the buffalo would not misbehave during the ceremony and slaughter.

The dancers performed around the buffalo, which was then ceremonially slaughtered in front of us. Well, not exactly. This time, the buffalo was spared. Today's dance was merely symbolic. But in the past, and at certain important events even now, the meat of the slaughtered beast was carved up, there and then, and the parts distributed appropriately between those entitled.

The dances continued until, during a pause, one of the men invited all the guests to participate in the next dance. We were encouraged, or in my case coerced. Dancing is not my forte. At parties I retreat into the shadows when the dancing begins. I feel awkward joining in, yet almost equally uncomfortable holding back, so today I acquiesced and did my best to follow the moves.

We watched the remainder of the performance from the *sopo*, the rice granary, opposite the Kings house, while Tiolina Sinambela elaborated on the program as it unfolded. She explained what each dance symbolized, while she shaded herself beneath a large dark blue parasol, lined inside with luscious red fabric, probably silk.

Afterwards we returned with Tiolina to the Glass House, her cosy home, where she opened a wooden chest full of her personal collection of ulos. These were exquisite and she let us feel and unfold them, holding them up for each other to see the wonderful designs.

To Batak, the ulos carries special symbolic value. An ulos is gifted on a special occasion, such as a birth, or a marriage. As such, it carries special value and significance to both the giver and the receiver. Kept, used, and valued throughout the owner's life, the colors may mellow, and the fabric may soften. The ulos is treated with reverence.

Kristin and I each bought a handwoven ulos from Tiolina. I chose a dark blue one, with a pale blue ikat batik pattern, which reminded me of moonlight catching the ripples on water. It had a dark blood-red border. The other, an older one from Tiolina's collection, was also blue and black. It was much softer, and the colors had comfortably mellowed with age.

Although much of Tiolina's collection was of museum quality, we were more interested in fabrics that we felt personally drawn to, ones we could use and enjoy, rather than fabrics we should hide away and preserve for posterity. Tiolina was a lovely warm woman, and we felt sad to leave her. As we were leaving, she asked us to wait for a moment. She ran back to her house and returned with a handwoven scarf, in soft pinks and purples, which she gave as a gift to Kristin, tenderly draping it around her neck. It was something Kristin would treasure.

We had spent our last Indonesian cash. On our way back we stopped to make a withdrawal at an ATM but failed. Cash is used for all transactions here except barter. With credit and debit cards rarely accepted, there are few places where cash may be withdrawn.

Liberta Hotel, where we stayed, is in a tourist village. Here we saw more European tourists and tourist shops than anywhere yet. We stopped for lunch at the Tabo Bakery. This lakeside restaurant was run by Annette Horschmann, another German woman married to a local man. Swina and Priyo recognized her, their having met before, and pointed her out. She was sitting at lunch with her family, and a dog, so we did not interrupt her meal.

This café had, understandably, a more European styling than any other place we had seen. It evidently caters well, with simple dishes, to tourists and expatriates. I happily indulged in fish and chips, which for me is comfort food. I seldom visit my childhood home, in the south of England, without stopping at a fish and chip shop near the seafront to pick up a meal wrapped in paper to take away.

Here, farther from the salt water, we sat in a circular pavilion in a landscaped area, well maintained and clean. The narrow grounds ran down to the corner of the lake where, in the dark last night, the ferry had spun unpredictably. It was interesting to view it from the opposite perspective.

The outdoor shelter, where we sat, was well appointed, with convenient electrical outlets. Our group did not miss the opportunity to plug in their phones and battery chargers, crowding together to use them even while they recharged. It was comfortable and modern compared to many other places at which we had eaten.

Tuk Tuk, like the neighboring villages on the mushroom-shaped peninsula, offers tourist accommodations and activities for overseas and domestic visitors. Small boats and ferries conveniently shuttle people back and forth, stopping at the waterfront properties. Everything seems ideally situated for visitors, yet tourism here peaked in 1996, with almost four million tourists. It has since declined, for several reasons.

First there was the disruption due to smoke from forest fires in 1997. Then, more recently, poor water quality, which was attributed to a surfeit of fish farms. Anoxia caused the death of millions of fish in some of the fish-farms in 2016 and 2018. Add to that a period of poor world economy, and politics, and it is easy to see why tourism declined.

The tragic demise of the ferry MV Sinar Bangun, which sank in bad weather between Parapat and Tomok in 2018, did little to inspire confidence. About 170 people were lost in that single disaster, most becoming trapped inside when the ferry went down. Due to the considerable depth of the lake, about five hundred meters (1,640 feet) where it sank, very few bodies could be recovered. Since most visitors reach Samosir Island by ferry, many must be mindful of that disaster, and some deterred.

Tuk Tuk today had the air of a tourist destination out of season, reminding me of wintertime at Brighton, England, where I grew up. Businesses were mostly empty and the streets quiet. When I thought about it, I realized that despite the weather which I found rather pleasant, late February is low season here just as in Brighton. Sure, Brighton sees cold rain, sleet or snow, and wild winds in February, rather than comfortably warm weather. Nevertheless, high season for Tuk Tuk is July and August the same as in Brighton.

Seasons aside, tourism has declined overall even in summer here. Recognizing that, measures are being taken to revive it. As a priority, the Indonesian government is improving road access. In addition, it plans to promote local sites, including geological, cultural, and scenic places of special interest. Related to that it has been applying for UNESCO status for some time, an asset in the promotion of the area.

At the time of writing, in July 2020, UNESCO added the Toba Caldera to the list of UNESCO Global Geoparks, considering the geological significance of the Toba Caldera, the traditional heritage and culture of the local communities, and the biodiversity.

To improve air quality, Indonesia wants to reduce the burning of forest lands, which may be one reason why tree cutting is followed by the spraying of chemicals to suppress forest regeneration in Lintong Forest.

To safeguard the drinking water quality of the lake, the government proposal is to reduce fish farming output to a maximum harvest of 10,000 tons of fish per year. The output is currently 40,000 tons per year. If that can be achieved, the tourist lake recreational activities that pollute least should also be encouraged over more polluting ones. Paddle-powered craft for example, solus, solus bolon, kayaks, with sailboats rather than jet-skis and powerboats.

I wonder to what extent local communities manage small-scale forest developments nowadays. Many of the resources needed by local communities, including materials and foodstuffs, come from species diverse forest, not from monoculture plantations. In the past centuries, Batak have utilized the forest, understanding how to sustainably harvest a multitude of resources from different species, while believing that spirits reside in individual trees and so respecting them.

I cannot see Indonesia establishing a policy to return eucalyptus plantations to species diverse forest anytime soon. But tree planting and forest maintenance could happen at a local level. Communities could play a part by growing native trees to both support wildlife and at the same time offer resources the community needs. Planting diverse species could support small scale businesses.

Rattan, a liana that relies on forest trees for support, is a versatile and valuable crop for furniture-making basketry and construction. In established forest it can be left to grow to the required diameter to be harvested when needed, or when the price is right. Indonesia already supplies most of the world's rattan, exporting raw materials. It is not yet focusing on finished products, which could be produced locally.

Frankincense and camphor, cassia, candlenut, mango and durian, timber for house construction and solus, materials for thatching, shade grown coffee and plants for dyes; the list of forest resources is considerable. Could community cooperatives maintain sustainable harvesting to utilize the many products they could derive from a diverse forest, in a relatively confined area?

Already the ulos is a marketable Batak product, sought after by tourists. How much more interesting would it for tourists to learn how the various species of trees, shrubs, and creepers, can be sourced for traditional dyes? It would also demonstrate the link between the environment and the cultural tradition.

In the afternoon, we used the cars to reach another historic village site, huta Siallagan, at the edge of Ambarita village. The Siallagans are descended from King Isumbaon, second son of King Batak, tracing the lineage back maybe nineteen generations.

The way into the huta from the street leads under an archway through a slot in the six-foot high wall of dressed rock. This passage is guarded on either side by a roughly carved, stern-faced stone statue. The wall, which fortifies this huta, is what remains of an even more effective defensive barrier that would have incorporated a deep bamboo hedge.

I turned to see where the stone figures were looking, and saw, across the narrow road, a lean-to shack, standing close to the high kerb. Banners advertising cigarettes dangled under the low front of the metal roof. A tobacconist, I wondered.

The front of the shop had been opened by folding back the wooden shutters, revealing a few columns of open plastic trays that held something, maybe snacks. A Coca-Cola cabinet displayed bottles of colored drinks, but anything else was hidden in the shade behind.

At the edge of the kerb, in front of what may have been another business under the same roof, stood a cooler with its wheels chocked. Stickers for soft drinks partially covered others advertising *Permalite*. Then I saw the green hose draped across the cooler, with the distinctive metal nozzle. Gasoline? Permalite, Indonesian gasoline. The penny finally dropped; this was a filling station.

The plot to the other side of the building was dedicated to a large blue and red painted tomb, rising in three tall layers, and topped with statues of three figures gazing out toward the lake. The lower two figures were seated, while the man on the top tier stood holding a staff.

I was still getting my bearings, but the others were ready to go in, so I turned and joined them, entering the village between the two stone-faced guards.

The courtyard stretching ahead was flanked on our left by the traditional houses, *rumah bolon*, many of which are still lived in. Opposite, along with the grain stores, *sopo*, were the sarcophagi of the ancestors. Dominating the courtyard part-way along grew a large tree, possibly the banyan *Ficus microcarpa*, with multiple trunks binding around each other and dripping with ferns and other epiphytes. Supporting it below, a tangled cylinder of stout knotted roots was confined within an encircling stone wall, filling it to the brim.

Beyond stood a platform with a circle of weathered stone chairs, often said to be two hundred years old, although everyone I asked seemed to have a different opinion of their age.

As I drifted from one building to another, admiring the carpentry, and the simplicity and beauty of the house construction, a guide urgently ushered us over to the seats and implored us to sit, and to role play.

"This stone seating area," he said, "is the place where the king, with his datu and important family members, would sit to determine the fate of captives."

"You should be the king," he suggested, indicating the seat of honor where I should sit. Kristin should sit beside me as my wife, or queen. Ade and Saleh should also sit as members of the same family. He would play the other roles, including that of the datu, and of the prisoner. First, he presented to each of us a narrow band of white, red, and black woven cloth to wear around our head or neck.

Prisoners were usually wrongdoers or captured enemy men. The captives would have been imprisoned beneath the house in the space normally reserved for keeping animals overnight. The prisoner, with hands tied behind his back, and one leg trapped in a heavy wooden stock, would not be fed, or otherwise cared for during captivity, which could be a week or much longer. When the datu thought the signs indicated an auspicious day for a trial, he was released from the leg stock and brought to the circle.

If found guilty, the convict would be taken to another stone table and blindfolded, to be tortured for hours. His flesh would be lacerated and marinated with lime juice, chili pepper and salt, and beaten to tenderize it. He would then be turned over for the treatment to continue. According to our guide, his tongue would be cut out, nose and cheeks cut off, and finally his head would be cut off. Any blood not drunk at that ceremony was used to paint the King's house.

After the king and his assembly had eaten the choicest parts, such as the palms of the hands, the soles of the feet, the cheeks and the heart, the remaining meat was eaten by the rest of the villagers, who were required to partake. The body parts and bones were thrown into the lake, which was avoided for a week or more afterward. The head was thrown up the mountain, from where, it was hoped, it would not be able to rejoin the rest of the remains of the body to return to haunt the village.

The gruesome story unfolded in a dramatic way, but it was hot sitting in the sun, and I noticed Kristin's eyelids drooping sleepily. The moment our guide finished his graphic narration of the trial and execution, he led us briskly by the arm toward the exit. Our group seemed to be the only visitors, and I wanted to spend more time to view the houses. But he was insistent, pushing us forward into the gauntlet of tourist souvenir stalls, a narrow and covered passageway that led toward the second village exit, and to freedom beyond the huta. From both sides, vendors called excitedly, waved, shouted, and beckoned, vying for attention.

Much as I realize how selling souvenirs is an essential part of the economy of tourist sites, these were not what I wanted to take home with me. Few things could deter me more from buying than overzealous sellers, that is, apart from the realization that I had spent my last Indonesian currency in the morning, and to buy anything required hard cash.

Priyo rescued me and we ducked into the crowded space beneath one of the houses. Sehat Siallagan, a good natured and handsome man used this low room, where a prisoner may have once been held, as a carving workshop. It was packed to overflowing with models and souvenirs he had made. He sat cross-legged on the floor behind his counter, while we crouched at a low bench opposite.

Sehat was eager to chat, speaking English well. He carved wooden models of houses which ingeniously folded open to reveal the inside, model solus with paddlers and paddles, and many other imaginatively devised pieces. Aged in his mid-sixties, he has been carving since the 1970s.

"The wood I use for carving," he disclosed, as he handed me a chunk to smell and examine, "is *ingul*, the same wood that is used for the solu, the dugout canoe."

This was the first I heard of this wood. Was not meranti the timber used for the solu?

Sehat said that ingul was a soft wood, good for carving, and weatherproof in that it was not affected by direct sun. It was resistant to rot even when not painted. "It is used for house construction too, where it is also carved."

"The black color of some of the carvings?" He smiled conspiratorially and showed us what he used for that. He winked. "Trade secret."

Later I discovered that ingul wood comes from the tree *Toona sinensis*, or Chinese mahogany. This tree grows to about twenty-five meters tall with a diameter of 70 cm (eighty-two feet tall, two feet four inches diameter). That would be an adequate size to build a solu, but surely not a solu bolon.

So, is Ingul a better timber than meranti for carving solus? Or is it that meranti is less available? The Simatupang family from the Muara district carved both solus bolon and solus from the meranti trees they found, but those trees were growing far away from lake Toba. Is Chinese mahogany more available, closer to the lake?

Back at the homestay, Pak Uli singled me out and invited me down to the water's edge. There he pulled together two chairs and produced a plastic bottle of tuak, inviting me to partake. I ran back for my mug, and then we sat and spent a pleasant hour in a calm back and forth. We shared the moment, watching a solu fisherman slowly circling his nets while methodically thrashing the water, the sound of the thumping splashes clearly audible from that distance.

Other guests strolled past us to view the evening lake, standing to admire the tranquil waterscape before moving on, or finding a place to sit. We chatted with one or two of the other guests, Pak Uli to Indonesians, me with a Dutchman who spoke English. All the while we sipped tuak, until the bottle was empty.

Pak Uli stood, signaling for me to stay where I was. He was gone for only a few minutes, returning with another full bottle of the milky liquid. Where he got his tuak from I do not know, but he always seemed to have a ready supply.

Pizza was on the menu that night, Priyo's plan being to walk to a restaurant at the eastern tip of Tuk Tuk. From the end of the lane, a narrow road wound uphill. We marched single file into the commercial zone, past small bars, illuminated shopfronts, and restaurants, all open to the street.

Most of the businesses were quiet, with just a few local people here and there, sitting at a café or a bar: seldom anyone who looked like a tourist. At our destination restaurant, we shared pizza and chips at a large round table, sipping beer. But when it was time to leave, we could hear the rumble of thunder, and wondered if we would be caught in a downpour.

Filing down the hill as the thunder rolled repeatedly, we reached the homestay replete, but sweaty in the humidity. We were indifferent to making music. Warned to be prepared for an early start tomorrow, our lackluster guitar playing ended early.

27. Mango Wine

I slid my kayak onto the water a little before the others were ready, gliding out onto the stillness. Alone, I had time to take in the sounds that rang clearly across the water from land, voices and bird calls, motors, and music. From nearby came the rhythmic splashing sound of a fisherman in a solu, whacking the water to startle the fish.

Looking back, I could see that Liberta, where we had stayed, was a traditional house, with a swooping metal roof, but with extensions clustered around it. That was a surprise to me. The warren of flanking additions, the open-walled library, dining, and lounge areas, masked that inner structure, hiding the distinctive Toba Batak building that I should have guessed was at its core.

Out here, several fishermen in solus tended their nets. Kingfishers sped above the water. Great clouds of white egrets with dark legs and bright yellow feet, twisted and drifted above the reed beds.

A small and almost empty passenger ferry sped toward shore, stopping briefly at the end of a narrow stone or concrete dock, Port Sosor Galung, between Liberta and the Tabo Bakery. It hovered, quietly churning water to hold the bow tightly to the cement wall. Water pumped rhythmically from a narrow pipe at the stern, the splash following each squirt audible above the gentle burbling of the motor.

Four or five passengers stepped up aboard, with backpacks. Then, as if making up for lost time, the boat reversed abruptly away. The engine note eased for a moment while the helmsman used the momentum to swing the bow, and then it shot forward toward Tomok.

Was this the same ferry that spun in wild circles playing loud music the night we arrived? Perhaps not, for although the location was the same, this more purposeful ferry, playing no music, seemed smaller.

Car ferries were leaving the shore from Tomok. Carrying just two or three cars, each was about half-full. They aimed away toward the east shore of the lake, presumably to Parapat, a little more than eight kilometers distant (5 miles).

From Parapat, visible from here beneath the steep shadowy green mountains, the road leads to Medan, the capital city of Sumatra, with its conurbation of 3.4 million people and its international airport. A bus leaves every hour from Parapat on the four to six-hour journey.

On this side, a few hundred meters inland from the Tomok ferry dock, should be the site of the tomb of King Sidabatar, where there are stone statues and ancient carved stone sarcophagi. We would not stop to visit these today, with thirty kilometers ahead (nineteen miles) to reach Onanrunggu. It was already 10.30. I for one was keen to arrive in plenty of time to see Mr. Omri Samosir's historic building in daylight.

Along the shore, rows of solus were beached just clear of the water. Each plastic solu in one group was painted a different bold color: bright red, green, yellow, or blue. Elsewhere were timber dugouts, true solus, each worth three of the plastic ones.

The wooden solus revealed their age. The newer they were, the brighter the wood. The older solus had darkened and weathered, the grain becoming more prominent. Some, scarred and cracked from constant use, had been painted and repainted. On those where much of the paint had worn or weathered away, it clung in patches, mostly in the cracks of the grain. The underlying colors showed here and there through the most recent coats, creating a colorful patina. Where one solu rested with its stern in the water, green algae furred the wood below the waterline.

What amazed me was the sheer number of these craft, especially considering that every solu I had seen afloat was either being paddled out to fish, being used for fishing, or returning from fishing. Such a fleet must take a toll on the wild fish population, as must the ubiquitous rod-fishing from shore.

Birds of prey hung above the reed beds, one clearly a Brahminy kite, known in Indonesia as *elang bondol,* with its rich light chestnut-colored back and pale head. I always felt uplifted when I saw these distinguished birds. They frequently flew in pairs, startling from a bush near shore when we were almost upon them. They would fly away low, their sunlit backs glowing a bright orange-brown, and their heads white.

They seldom flew far, just a little way ahead of us before taking perch again. Always keeping within our easy line of sight, they sometimes led us forward like this for twenty minutes at a time. My eyes became accustomed to following the gliding birds until the chestnut plumage folded into standstill. Then I kept watch on each motionless spot until the shadowy shapes blossomed into flight again.

Once we had all gathered, Priyo, Kristin, me and Saleh and Ade, we paddled on past rows of empty tour boats parked along the shore with their bows to the beach. They all exhibited a similar style with several fancy decks. Almost every hull was painted blue, but many colors decorated the superstructures. Why so many inactive? Granted, this is not the height of the tourist season, but there has been a fall in demand for these boats since the sinking of MV Sinar Bangun.

Not all the boats were idle, however. Two wooden cargo vessels sat waiting with engines running, one almost fully loaded, the other only partially.

The first, its gunwales boarded up higher with blue-painted planks to better secure its load, was shaded by a torn cloth canopy. Onshore, men hoisted bulky white sacks of fish food from a stack outside a warehouse near the water. Taking one or two at a time on their heads, shoulders, or backs, they hurried down to the dock and stepped aboard at the bow. They squeezed aft past the wheelhouse to find a place to drop their load. The men hastened despite the heat, in a continuous cycle, like a stream of ants carrying crumbs.

When the first boat neared capacity, with sacks stacked on board five or six high, the final sacks were heaped onto the bow. Everyone boarded, and the boat immediately pulled away from shore.

Now the men reclined, or sat on the bulging sacks, lighting up cigarettes, enjoying a brief sojourn. In a few minutes time they would be back at work offloading all the cargo onto the floating platforms that surround the fish enclosures. We could see platforms smothering the water just a few hundred meters offshore. Each platform appeared to have a tiny square hut, for storing fish food, or for keeping guard.

There were nets everywhere here too, even between the fish farms and the shore. Close to shore, strung between dark ring floats, or beneath sealed plastic bottles commandeered for the same purpose, the nets drooped down in loose curtains of silvery nylon threads. We passed fishermen in solu after solu all along the coast, each one circling to check nets or lifting traps. It must be an inhospitable place for a fish, and a challenge to navigate a boat anywhere here without snagging a net. Maybe it is easier to use a paddle-powered solu than a motorboat.

Close on shore, buildings were going up. Some might become quite large resorts by local standards, but nothing appeared to rise more than two or three storeys. Built up square in a Western style with concrete or brick walls and glass windows, they morphed above into traditional Toba Batak architectural forms. Here were the generous overhanging eaves beneath elegant swooping rooflines. But no matter how large the buildings, the backdrop of green hills rising 760 meters (2,500 feet) close behind, dwarfed all the coastal development.

Saleh checked his cell phone frequently, dropping way back, but with the power of a bull he quickly caught up each time. Priyo paddled strongly with his beloved carbon Greenland paddle. Kristin accompanied me, skimming along happily as the strengthening wind behind kicked up waves big enough for us to ride.

It was a low shore, but each time we rounded a headland we cut closer to the steep high slope; the backbone that runs like a wall along this side of the island. Each minor headland we rounded revealed the next, just a short distance ahead. Each time I thought I would see the steep slope right at the shore, instead it kept tantalizingly just out of reach. We ever-so-gradually converged, but as we did, the elevation of that spine diminished.

Already well past midday, a woman waved and called to us from the deck of what looked like a guest house and restaurant. I waved back, unable to hear what she was saying. The name of the place was painted on the seawall, in red capital letters on a yellow background, along with a white painted crossed spoon and fork, and an icon of a bed under a roof. Maybe she wanted us to dine or stay there.

"Could you hear what she said?" I asked Kristin.

"Not really," she replied, "but I think it was something about mangoes." Priyo had not mentioned any plans to stop at a restaurant, and we were being swept quickly past. Just in case the woman could hear us in the wind, we shouted back out, "Horas! Horas! Horas!" and then sped on, enjoying the rhythm of the lake. Riding on the waves, we kept up a brisk and easy speed. It was wonderfully sensuous.

Caught up in the energy of the water, we sped past a fisherman casting from shore with a rod, and a group of women gathering mangoes. A nest of children erupted when they saw us, shouting and leaping. Surfing around a corner into calm we found ourselves in front of a house, with people getting to their feet to call and wave. The whole shore was seemingly alive with hidden or semi hidden people.

Vaguely hearing a whistle, I thought nothing of it, but when it blew again, I became alert and stopped to look. It was then that we spotted Priyo coming after us, waving for us to stop.

We sat and drifted, watching an osprey turn overhead. It circled more rapidly, into tighter and tighter turns while losing altitude. Then it swooped down at speed toward where an egret stood. I was riveted. Would an osprey go for an egret?

There was a commotion when the two big birds met, a fluster of thrashing wings. Then the egret flew off low above the water along the shore, legs trailing. The osprey had not caught the egret. But when the raptor climbed with heavy wingbeats, aiming onshore, we saw it carried a fish in its claws. Had it snatched the fish from under the egret's watchful eye, or had it stolen the egret's catch? I could not tell. Either way, the osprey got a fish.

When Priyo reached us, he told us everyone had spontaneously decided to stop for lunch. The others were back there, where we had seen the woman waving from her deck. It was lunch time anyway, he said, and it was a good reconnaissance opportunity. "Did you not see her wave," he asked? "We should head back."

I regretted that Priyo had been put to all that trouble just to stop us. But I was grateful to him. It took us 20 to 25 minutes of vigorous paddling against the wind to regain the small beach where the other kayaks sat. Our escort boat was moored at the shore.

There was the heavy sweet smell of mango in the air when we scrambled up the awkward wall from the beach to the path by the house. There we found two boys, in green knee-high rubber boots, laughing as they stomped inside what looked like the stainless-steel drums from washing machines. They were pounding their feet to squash mangoes underfoot. One took a bite from a sandwich he held in his hand and chewed as he worked. Gradually the viscous juice oozed through the holes, the orange-colored liquid pooling underneath in a rough tray lined with a heavy polythene sack. This juice, they explained excitedly, would be fermented to make mango wine.

We left them to their aromatic squishing and scaled the steep and tall, orange-tiled steps to the house. We had arrived at the Silimalombu Ecovillage, where the owner of the complex, Ratnauli Gultom or *Ratna* for short, managed a restaurant, homestay, and farm. Gultom was the family name of Sitor Situmorang's first wife, Iman's mother.

Ratna was self-confident in her manner, and proud of her achievements here. She was Indonesian, she said, and Thomas, her husband, was German. Their visitors today, some of whom were volunteers, or interns, included a group of Germans and a Hungarian girl. We skirted one group of them seated casually around a dining table, chatting over empty coffee cups. More of them stood working at a tall island counter in the kitchen. Finally, we found our own group relaxing on the covered terrace.

There stood low tables, made from dugout canoes each about three meters long (eight feet). The tabletops were cut from thick clear plexiglass. When I admired them, Ratna said that she had carved them herself and made them into tables. She lounged back proudly on an armchair constructed of short logs of hefty bamboo, tied in such a way that they shifted and conformed comfortably under load. This chair, like others around us, and a longer couch, were of her own design and construction. Ratna had hurt her leg, which affected her posture as she sat on that throne of a chair looking regal. A guitar hung on the wall behind her, between two big glass windows which let light into a room behind.

Ratna explained how she and Thomas practiced self-sufficiency, commune style, growing all that they needed. They set up some hydroponics, with the plastic pipes latticing the wall of the terrace. With so many mango trees, and so much fallen fruit, they decided to make mango wine with the surplus. Clearing the ground of fallen fruit around the trees helps to control the spread of insect pests that can otherwise afflict the next harvest.

Ratna also grew and packaged candlenuts, and pressed candlenut oil. Growing around were also durian, coconut, cacao, cinnamon, soursop, and guava. It was Ratna's father who founded the village, so she was the daughter of the King of Silimalombu. Many of the men living there worked on the fish farms, while the women caught wild lake fish, and crayfish.

Several people sat tasting mango wine on the covered terrace, pouring from bottles of three different types and comparing the merits of each. The wine was for sale in little bottles on display near a big central counter. There, several people now sat on tall stools, or stood aside, sampling food while others cooked.

Our group had spread around loosely beside the solu tables either sitting on the floor or on stools, short heavy stumps of debarked and varnished tree trunk. They were eating lunch. Tandon and Ally, who had finished, lounged in a recliner, another of Ratna's bamboo log constructions.

The three of us, Priyo, Kristin and me, were still dripping wet from splashing our way back against the wind. I unwrapped my packed lunch of rice, fish, chicken, and sambal, wondering how to eat it with my fingers without spreading a mess.

Ratna, bubbly and welcoming, offered each of us a shot-glass of home-made, avocado-mango smoothie. It was rich and fruity. She also encouraged us to sample the mango wines, one of which tasted like a dry sherry, another more like a heavy dessert wine.

"Make yourselves coffee if you would like." she offered. "You will find everything at the other end of the kitchen. Just help yourself."

There, Thomas cut his fresh-baked bread, and mango strudel too, and invited us to sample both. His baking was wonderful, and a change from the usual Indonesian cooking. At the counter, by a bowl of fresh casava noodles, a young man shredded blocks of fresh pasta into fettuccini.

We recognized one of the women as someone we had seen before but had not been introduced. She was Annette Horschmann, the German woman who owned the café Tabo Bakery and Cottages at Tuk Tuk where we lunched yesterday. She apologized for not having taken time to speak with us before but made up for it today. She was here with her Indonesian husband. They were both good friends of Ratna and Thomas. Her son, she pointed him out, was here visiting from Germany with his girlfriend, the Hungarian girl.

Having encountered more than a few people of German origin living around here, I was beginning to see a pattern. Nommensen and the German missionaries probably sowed an awareness of Lake Toba in Germany. Although Germans may not have felt welcome here just after the Second World war, when Holland was trying to re-establish colonial control, that was certainly not the case now. German influence comes into Toba Batak life at a personal level. The Dutch and Japanese seem to have made more of an overall structural impact.

Our colorful kayaks sat on the beach just above the waterline. In the summer of 2012, there was a massive earthquake off the coast of Sumatra. Unlike the earthquake that caused the devastating tsunami of 2004, this was a strike-slip quake. That kind of earthquake is caused by a horizontal slip, like two books flat on a table with their spines sliding against one another. Without an up-thrust, there was no big tsunami. However, it was the largest such quake ever recorded by instrument: the tenth largest quake overall in the previous hundred years.

Yet this earthquake set up a seiche in lake Toba. A seiche, sometimes described as being tsunami-like, is experienced as a series of surface oscillations, like water slopping to and fro in a bucket. At the shore it is seen like the rise and fall of the tide, but on a faster timescale.

Here at Silimalombu there was a vertical rise and fall of about one meter (three feet), as each of a succession of slow, surging, waves reached up the shore. Solus and boats all along the island shore were lifted afloat and carried out onto the lake. The whole of the beach where our kayaks sat high and dry was inundated up to waist deep, and something similar would have happened all around the lake.

Sumatra lies along the ring of fire, the horseshoe shaped series of tectonic plate boundaries around the Pacific Ocean. The ring of fire is particularly prone to earthquakes and volcanic eruptions. Indonesia lies along one of the more active parts in this respect.

The Indo-Australian tectonic plate moves at about six centimeters (2.5 inches) per year against the Eurasian plate. This plate boundary comprises about 5,000km (3,100 miles) of subduction zone. Along Sumatra, the pressure of one plate against the other is not directly opposed but is at an angle.

The Sumatran Trench, some 200-250km from shore (125-150 miles), is where the Indo-Australian plate pushes down under the Eurasian plate. As it dives, it creates an accretion zone parallel to the coast, which accounts for the island chain offshore western Sumatra.

The pressure also causes the edge of the Eurasian plate to buckle up, creating the mountain chain parallel to the trench. As the land buckles, it cracks along a series of geological faults. The two plates pressing at an oblique angle build up stresses, which are relieved from time to time by strike-slip earthquakes along the fault lines. It was one such strike-slip earthquake that caused the seiche here in 2012.

The series of faults along the line of the mountain chain are known together as the Great Sumatran Fault.

As the Indo-Australian plate subducts to a depth of around 100km (60 miles), the water carried down in the rock lowers the fusion point of the surrounding rock, creating magna. Less dense and hotter than the surrounding rock, this begins to rise like a bubble in a lava lamp. This is what causes volcanoes. Owing to the angle of subduction of the Indo-Australian plate, the volcanoes appear in a line along the Great Sumatran Fault, approximately 300km from the trench (180 miles).

The Indian Ocean earthquake of 2004, the third largest earthquake ever recorded, was caused by a rupture, or slip of about fifteen meters (50 feet) along some 1,600km (1,000 miles) of the Sumatran Trench, where the Indo-Australian plate subducts the Eurasian plate. It was the large vertical displacement of several meters over such a long fault line which generated the devastating tsunamis. Waves up to thirty meters high (one hundred feet) inundated the shore.

Resuming our journey, we reached the place where we had turned back with Priyo. Hours had since passed, yet here again was the osprey, circling over the water. This must be its usual hunting territory, the place it belongs. This time there was no egret.

28. The King's House

The low coast became narrower as the steep spine of the island finally reached the shore. We saw fewer houses, and then finally the only space for building was right at the shore. Almost hidden by trees, the southernmost few structures were threatened by overhanging crags higher up the steep slopes.

Beyond these final buildings there was no beach at all, as the slopes morphed into cliffs. We explored close beneath the rock, probing into clefts, and into a shallow cave. Then, looking up, we spotted a long-necked lizard, about a meter long, climbing slowly down the vertical wall. It examined the rock to one side and the other with the extra reach of its head, flicking its long blue tongue, before slowly insinuating itself into a crack. There was something otherworldly about the length of its neck that made its head movements look creepy.

This was the first Southeast Asian water monitor, *Varanus salvator,* that I had seen on this trip. Of all the species of lizard in the world, including the seventy-five or more different types of monitor, the Southeast Asian water monitor is the second heaviest, after the Komodo dragon. It can reach lengths of three meters (ten feet), so although this one was impressive, it was just a small one. Bigger ones can pose a danger to livestock and to little children.

Traditional Toba Batak houses often display carved lizards on the façade. The carvings can be large and prominent, but they represent the house lizard, which is small, and typically lives in or around houses. The house lizard is a symbol of fertility and of tenacity.

The lizard, as mentioned earlier, figures in Batak creation mythology. Raja Odapodap was born lizard-like. His hideous appearance was the reason why the two sisters were repulsed and escaped, the first becoming the sugar palm: her younger sister Sideak Parujar descending on her thread to earth. Since all the people on earth derive from Raja Odapodap and Sideak Parujar, the lizard is a mythical ancestor of all Batak.

An ability to adopt a disguise, to change appearance, chameleon-like, is shared by the rare lizard species *Harpesaurus modiglianii*. One specimen was found by Italian naturalist Elio Modigliani, when exploring around Lake Toba in 1891. The specimen he found was dead, but notable for its flattened nose horn, which projects forward, rather than rhino-like, upward.

This new species was named after Modigliani, along with four other species, including a frog first found in the Lake Toba area, *Huia modiglianii.*

Modigliani's dead lizard specimen was a bluish color, so it was thought the species color was blue. Instead, it turned out that the color was an effect of the preserving alcohol. It was not until 2018 that another dead specimen was found near Lake Toba. Further searches turned up live specimens. The color of the live lizard is bright fluorescent lime green, with a spiky line of upright dorsal crest plates, also green. When threatened, *Harpesaurus modiglianii* camouflages to a brownish color, with bright orange crest plates.

We waited under the cliff, hoping our monitor would reappear, but we saw no more of it.

Plants hung in curtains, sometimes as thickets of roots, other times as tangles of creepers that we ducked or dodged around. We surfed around corners close to the rock, enjoying our proximity to the steep cliffs. Below were deep dark depths. Water slapped into hollows and rustled as it lapped the walls beside us. This was the most dramatic section of the east coast. Streams cascaded down cool dark corners of rock, clattering into tight gullies.

When the gradient finally became less steep, we saw houses clustered at the shore again. We shouted, "Horas!" as we passed families on shore, and men in solus. Gangs of small children leaped up and down excited, waving and calling.

We paused for a while at the shore beneath the site of what Priyo thought was the oldest Muslim tomb on Samosir. He said he heard the story of how it was a tomb for two people, travelers, or traders, visiting the area. He did not think they were from here, and he said they died a long time ago.

I was eager to reach Onanrunggu and felt impatient when we all stopped at a mosque beside the water. People stood talking in the entrance porch which was supported by dark green pillars. This was a modest green square building with a pyramidal corrugated metal roof, topped with a circular lookout with glazed windows. All was crowned with a silvered onion dome. The trumpet of a speaker was mounted below the lookout for the call to prayer.

Saleh landed on the narrow sandy beach and scrambled up the steep sandbank, past the wild shrubs with yellow blossoms, to talk with the men on shore about the mosque. Meanwhile, we rested in our kayaks, bobbing gently by the beach.

Our direction had gradually changed as we rounded the southeast end of Samosir Island. We followed the shore now in the general direction of the distant Sibandang Island, although we would not go that far. I could also see the misty bay, some twenty kilometers away (twelve miles), where we had stopped at Bakara on our route north. Now we had all but rounded

Samosir Island. The distant features of the rim of the caldera appeared like layers of shade, each more remote skyline bluer and hazier. Sheltered here from the wind, the lake seemed to relax. The waves had dropped.

Our destination today was little more than two kilometers away (a mile). It was a beach, by a rough stone jetty under construction, near some low houses. As I landed, women crowded around me, chattering. They questioned me even as I lifted my kayak by the bow to float it ashore, but I could not understand their questions, nor they mine. Suddenly, one woman broke into a broad smile and roared, "Selfie!" All the other women laughed, and came hurrying over, jovial, and friendly.

We all squeezed together into the frame while one took a picture, and then again, and again, as more women crowded in, pulling out their cellphones. Others called for them to wait, running to join in.

With the way clear, our support boat pulled carefully up against the side of the dock and began unloading everything into the pickup and car. Both had reversed up as close as possible. We lifted our kayaks from the sandy shore, away from the solus parked there, to a slender tree, to unload them just distant enough from all the activity and inquisitiveness at the shoreline.

The kayaks emptied, we secured the cockpits and turned each kayak inward one against the next in a stack to make them less conspicuous. Somehow, it seemed unlikely anyone would tamper with them, or borrow them without asking. Then, walking behind the slow-moving cars, we ambled, wearily, about 350 meters (four hundred yards) inland along narrow dusty roads to reach Onanrunggu, the village of Mr. Omri Samosir's family.

There, from a gate in the cyclone fencing, spread a generous alaman, or lawn as it appeared, between two rows of houses.

With short grass, not packed earth, it was evident that nowadays this huta saw little foot traffic. On the south side, both traditional houses and modern houses stood in a row, including the most impressive, elaborately decorated, Kings house. Behind these were more buildings among trees. Low smart modern houses, with tiled covered terraces, stood opposite on the north side of the alaman where granaries would have stood.

Here again was the basic village layout Iman impressed upon me. This alaman runs east-west, so each house is aligned with the entrance facing north. The morning light shines along the field from the east, and the setting sun illuminates the field from the west end. But never does the sun beat directly onto the front or back of the houses, where it could heat them. It only hits the overhanging roofs, now metal, but once covered in palm fiber thatch. The thatch would have insulated well from the sun's heat. Aligned like this, the houses stayed cool.

Now we could see the King's House where we would sleep, the spectacular structure built here before any European ever saw Lake Toba. Outside, the wooden walls were decorated with ornate carvings all around, painted in white, red, and black. As was typical, the whole house was one room, standing high on its stout timber supports.

Up inside was more like a cave than a room: cool and calm with time-darkened wood. Mats covered the wooden floor, with two rows of mattresses lined up for all of us to sleep on. Kristin and I dropped our bags to claim the space beside the substantial wooden king's treasure chest, in the back corner on the west side. This chest once doubled as the sleeping place for the king, who would sleep on top of the sturdy lid. The design of the chest mirrored that of the middle layer of a house, with the long, boat-shaped beams along each side. It also mirrored the shape of a huta, bound within its long defensive walls.

Two girls suddenly appeared through a small rear entrance carrying pillowcases and sheets for us. I was startled, having mistaken the little opening for a window. Now, looking down from it, I saw the steep steps, or fixed ladder.

I climbed down to a concrete courtyard, with other houses on one side part-hidden by trees. A clothes rack in the sun offered us opportunity to dry our kayaking garments. On the other side was a low concrete building with a toilet, and sometimes running water.

Dinner was soon served on the covered terrace of the house across the alaman, the dishes being prepared in the house beside the King's house and carried across. Shedding our shoes to step up onto the immaculate mirror-clean tiled floor, we found a table spread with steaming pots of rice, fish, chicken, and soup. There were hot and spicy sambals as condiments, and hot coffee. Helping ourselves, we carried our laden plates to sit, on chairs, at tables, all choosing to face outward in a row. Our view was of the magnificent house where we would sleep, its façade ornately carved and painted, embellished with a buffalo motif at the front crest of the roof, and a symbolic buffalo tongue motif stretching down toward the balcony where a row of drums hung.

To the left of the King's house stood a low modern building, and beside that, two traditional houses. The latter were smaller than the King's house, compact, cosy shapes that made me think of house boats. They were more roughly built, without carved decoration. A simple ladder led up at the front of one. There was no ladder to the other, but patina showed where one used to be.

As darkness crept up from the shadows around the buildings, the fading daylight withdrew upward into the sky. Then lights sprang on to spotlight the façade of the Kings house, bringing the intricately textured surfaces into relief.

I sat content in my own world, quietly munching, savoring the moment. Around me, the low earnest conversation in Bahasa Indonesia occasionally bubbled into laughter. Beside me, Kristin drew my attention to the food, asking me if I recognized a certain detail, or had tasted this dish, or that spice.

I finished my meal. Collecting up empty plates, pouring and handing out coffee, looking out at the scene, I wondered how different it would have been here a generation ago, or two, or three. What would life have been like on February evenings before the Dutch arrived? What was it like here, at Onanrunggu, under Dutch rule, as daylight faded into night?

With my thoughts drifting to times gone by, I was in for a culture shock. In the middle of the courtyard, halfway between the King's house and the house where we sat, a large mat was unrolled and spread over the grass. A black car reversed from between the houses opposite, stopping near the mat. Two people lifted a heavy dark box from the back of the car and positioned it beside the mat. The driver plugged an electrical lead into the box, and an extension cord to that. She then unwound the long cord, dragging the free end away across the grass toward the building by the King's house.

Powered on, the heavy dark box, with its big speaker on the front, flashed frenetically with bright colored lights. We all gathered there as it began to stream music from a cellphone. Everything was set up for karaoke!

Once we were all grouped together on the mat, Swina took up a cordless microphone. She looked around, delighted to be the MC. Her amplified voice purred as she explained how she had arranged this as a surprise. Only now, almost at the end of our trip, did we discover how much she loved to sing.

Swina sang the first song, dedicating it to Kristin and me, and then sang on, solo, and with Priyo. They performed well together. More songs then followed, sometimes in Bahasa Indonesia, otherwise in English, with styles ranging from Frank Sinatra to the Beatles. Everyone who knew the song lyrics, or could find them, joined in the singing, or tried to. People scrolled to read; their faces illuminated by their glowing cellphones.

The music beat on at full speed, challenging everyone's ability to read lyrics from a tiny screen in a foreign language, fast enough to keep up. There were charming mispronunciations, ad libs, and hanging pauses in the vocals, while the music hurried on regardless. Some joined in heartily with a recognizable line, or a chorus, but held back on the less familiar sections, so the singing volume swelled and faded unpredictably.

As each song finished, there came a burst of suggestions, and requests, and discussion. Ghost faces appeared again as screen-illuminated fingers scrolled to locate song titles. Ready, someone else took hold of the microphone to lead the next song. But suddenly, the music hiccoughed and stopped. It was likely some hitch with the karaoke machine, or a poor phone connection not streaming smoothly. Another song almost immediately broke up. A third song was aborted.

Failing to get the karaoke machine working smoothly again, we went acoustic. Tandon took up the guitar to accompany, while Priyo sang. Tandon, both an accomplished guitarist, and a good singer, was happy to play while others sang, but reluctant to play and sing simultaneously.

When the guitar passed around, I discovered Swina could play guitar too. Priyo, Tandon, Syahrul and I then each took turns. It brought us all together.

When at last nobody reached for the guitar, we fell silent and flopped onto our backs on the mat, hoping to see the stars. Although we could point out and name the main constellations, and spot the steadily moving satellites, the lights on the buildings proved too bright for a good night view of the sky. The sky had been more scintillating when seen from the water.

In the morning, I lay awake at around 6:30 in the cool, dark, quiet of the old house. It was comforting and cozy, looking up into the high-pitch roof with its battens and sweeping beams. Far from it seeming spooky here last night, I felt soothed and safe when we climbed up into the cavern, our flickering headlamps illuminating a corner here, or the high reach of the roof. The air was fresh, with the slightly aromatic smokiness of old timber. It was a very calm space.

With the early-golden sun casting long shadows and conjuring sparkling jewels from the dew-adorned grass, we strolled wet-footed across the alaman to a leisurely buffet breakfast on the veranda of the house opposite. There we sat facing outward once again to savor the sight of the magnificent carved façade of the King's house, feeling more affinity having slept there.

29. Paddling a Solu

Having hoped to meet the solu craftsman who lived not far from here, I was disappointed to hear he was not at home this morning. Over the phone he told Mr. Omri Samosir that we were welcomed to try a solu he left on the beach. Excited to paddle it, I hurried to save enough time to do so before we departed.

At the beach, our kayaks loaded and ready, Saleh identified the correct solu from among several there. It was short, cut from a single log. Whether it was carved from ingul, or meranti, I could not tell without asking the builder, but it was heavy.

This solu, like most others I had seen on Lake Toba, was highly rockered, the hull curving upward towards the ends like a banana, with almost vertical sides and flattish bottom. There was a small square deck at the bow and stern, reinforced underneath by a vertical support that resembled a rudder, all part of the same log. Under the deck, the bow and stern were full and rounded, but would remain out of the water, unless the waves were big. It was beautifully shaped, with pleasing symmetry.

As a kayak designer, I found it conceptually interesting to examine a boat created by taking material away. Most boats nowadays are made by adding material, often piece by piece, but seldom by removing it, piece by piece. I was reminded of the time when, working with the American kayak manufacturer Liquidlogic, I watched Allen Stancil, designer of the legendary *Dancer* whitewater kayak of 1982, carve a kayak plug from a block of high-density foam. First marking out some lines with a felt tipped marker pen, he picked up a chainsaw to begin the shaping.

I imagine the outside of this solu must have been shaped first, determining the performance on the water. The inside would be carved to offer more cargo space, or less, with care taken not to cut through the hull. The thickness of the hull varied from one place to another, a consequence of how it was hollowed out: one shape on the inside, a different shape on the outside.

When I sat in the solu on the low wooden seat, I felt quite tippy, so I moved the seat aside and sat on my shoes instead. With my center of gravity lowered, I felt more stable. The more wood the builder carved from the bottom, the lower the possible center of gravity and stability of the paddler. But to sit on the bottom would be to sit in water, so the hull should be carved deep enough to accommodate a seat.

Gingerly, I paddled from shore, finding this solu handled much like a solo whitewater open canoe; every bit as maneuverable, but tippier. The paddle, which was longer and heavier than I am used to, felt clumsy. The blade, dipping deep into the water, suddenly caught tight in the weeds. Clinging to it for a moment too long, I was lucky to avoid falling in.

As I unwrapped the weed from the blade, one of our kayaks raced past. Paddling it, a local woman beamed at me with the biggest smile of glee. I felt no less joyful, if tentative by comparison. While she sped confidently onward, I focused on balancing and keeping my blade clear of the weed.

Fishermen along the Samosir shore hang their nets in the shallows around the weed beds where the fish shelter. They must constantly have to avoid snagging the paddle. I abandoned my J stroke to try other options.

Sculling, with just one hand on the paddle, I managed better. Pinning the shaft through the crook of my elbow, and against my shoulder, the way the fishermen do, I could circle easily in either direction without catching the weeds. With the blade closer to the surface than before, I could also scoot forward in a straight line without catching the weeds.

Curious about the paddle, I could only deduce based on what I saw. Firstly, every paddle that I had held was heavy but strong. Sturdy is good, although the weight is of no advantage. It is probably the consequence of the type of wood, plus some absorbed water in the absence of waterproofing.

Like many others I saw, this paddle was long, with no handle at the end. When using only one hand, a handle is unnecessary, so why not have a shaft long enough to serve when standing? Then, when sitting, the required leverage can be found by holding the shaft in the same way as a kayak paddle and moving the hands up or down the shaft.

This solu was doubtless carved for a smaller paddler than me, someone with a lower center of gravity. I wondered who chose the dimensions. Did the builder size up the paddler to carve a boat for them, or did the paddler try out different boats to choose the one most suitable? Or was it random, determined by the size of the log? I had nobody to ask.

Kristin tried next and paddled the solu smoothly. As she cruised around and practiced maneuvering, a boat, heavily laden with a cargo of creamy colored, angular boulders of what looked like limestone, approached the dock. Indonesian pop music jangled above the noise of the thudding engine. Two of the crew jumped ashore with lines. A third scrambled around the narrow decks, a cigarette dangling from his mouth. He probed the water with a long bamboo pole and pushed against the bottom to edge the boat closer alongside. Waiting for the slow-following wakes to steepen in the shallow water, Kristin accelerated to ride a wave back to shore.

Priyo began his turn in the solu, fighting for balance like a man on a rodeo horse, gradually finding stability and composure. While I watched, I reflected how I would have enjoyed comparing solus of different dimensions, learning more about how they are designed and built, and comparing how they performed. I was most grateful for the opportunity to try this one. I would have loved to paddle it for longer, but since our support boat and the other paddlers had already left, we drained and parked the solu, jumped into our kayaks and followed.

30. Closing the Circle

Having almost completed our circumnavigation of Samosir Island, our new target was a peninsula on the east side of the lake. The coastal cliffs, rising as much as 450 meters (1,200 feet) above the lake, curved north as scree slopes of creamy-yellow rock. Priyo described how that steep coast was continually crumbling, shifting, and falling. When previously exploring that section, he had kept offshore to avoid all the falling rocks.

"There is nowhere safe to land along there," he explained. "That is one of the reasons I chose this route around Samosir Island."

That unstable stretch is the edge of the collapsed portion of the original caldera rim, which dropped into the crater before the lake filled, breaking away along a fracture line farther east. That eastern limit of the collapsed portion can be seen set back from the coast several kilometers inland, across the Uluan Peninsula, as the steep scarp rising a thousand meters (three thousand feet) above the plateau.

If the Uluan peninsula appears somewhat level with long ridges, it is because the land cracked along lines from northeast to southwest, and the blocks of land settled down against one another in tilted block faulting.

We finally reached the mainland shore at a narrow cove with large, rounded rocks standing from the water and lurking below. It was overhung by trees, and the water between the big rocks was deep and cloudy, with many fish. I watched the boat approach, cautiously reversing, maneuvering, and taking its time to avoid the boulders, looking for a place where it could safely float close enough to moor. Once the engine was stilled, I could hear the birdsong ringing out noisily from the forest above our heads.

Now everyone jumped into the water to swim; Tandon with his camera, filming from the water, trying to follow Ally who slid through the water like a fish.

Perched on a rock, with my feet on my kayak to keep it from drifting away, I unwrapped my lunch. Today I found a huge portion of rice, chicken which was sinewy-tough, and a sharp-boned fish. Of course, there was plenty of spicy sambal sauce too. I tried to eat cleanly with my fingers, but rice kept escaping. Those morsels, falling between the rock and my kayak, drifted down into the hazy water toward a shoal of little fish. Was I getting any better at eating rice with my fingers? I suspected not.

Hermann Norden in 1923 referred to a meal at a huta, where chicken and rice were swiftly prepared and just as quickly eaten.

The missionary ate his rice Batak fashion. He squeezed it into a ball in his fist, dipped it in the gravy and swallowed it. No fork was needed.

Describing a meal in Sumatra, the American missionary Munson lamented his own inadequate skill at eating that way.

...where, served with curry and rice, but no knives forks or spoons, we were therefore compelled to resort to the Malay method of eating, with our fingers.

The rest of the company having been longer in the country, succeeded well; but I could not acquire the necessary sleight of hand. Fortunately, I had been amusing myself with conchology, by collecting a few shells on the beach. So, taking the half of a bivalve, I finished my supper without further difficulty.

I too might have eaten more cleanly with a shell today. I should have thought to carry a spoon.

The rough rattling beat of a motor caught my attention. It heralded the approach of another boat carrying a cargo of stone rubble from the direction of the scree slopes. As the noise of the engine grew more deafening, so all the birds in the forest around the bay seemed to sing especially loudly. Once the boat had passed, the singing stopped again, or at least was stilled to a murmur. A few minutes later I heard the approach of another boat, also carrying stone rubble. Again, the birds ramped up their chorus. Where was all the rock coming from, and where was it going? There was such a steady stream of boats. Maybe the stone that was being offloaded at Onanrunggu earlier came from the same place.

Farther along the shore the water grew shallow, with pale bleached water weed covered in slime. It seemed unhealthy. Whether it was a result of the boat traffic, construction along the shoreline, or contamination from the fish farms, it was certainly the worst water quality I had seen in the lake.

The lake's only outlet lay eleven kilometers from here (seven miles) at the end of the bay that hooked to the northeast, in the direction the boats laden with rocks were bound. From there, Lake Toba drains down the 150km long (90 miles) Asahan River to the Malacca Strait. Since dammed above a steep gorge by the Sigura-gura dam, to regulate water flow for hydroelectric power, the section of whitewater below the dam is world-renowned among serious whitewater kayakers.

Our often quietly brooding driver, Syahrul, makes his living on this whitewater river, organizing events, instructing, and leading whitewater paddlers. When I see him withdrawn in quiet contemplation, I often wonder if he is dreaming of paddling whitewater, bored with watching us cruise around on the flat lake. I can imagine him calmly negotiating the rapids while the songs of Creedence Clearwater Revival run like a mantra through his head. Risk averse as a driver, he made us feel safe on the road, as I expect he would inspire our confidence on whitewater.

Instead of following the coast around past the lake exit, we crossed directly to the nearest point of land, to the northwest of Baligé. There we connected our lake loop, retracing our route past the wooden ship under construction and past familiar buildings.

As this would be our last paddling day, I felt reluctant to rush. I wanted to savor the experience, take in as much as I could of the view, and contemplate a little. I paused to view a small cottage close to the water.

Like many we saw, it was not a traditional house. Yet it had been built four steps up above the ground, over an open framework of beams, in a similar manner to the big houses. That left a crawl space a little more than a meter tall under the house. The floorplan was rectangular, no larger than a single room, with an even smaller lower addition at the back with its own side door, and a lean-to behind that. In front was an entrance hall just half the width of the house, with a pitched roof and the door to one side.

The walls were a patchwork of horizontal boards set edge to edge, except for the eaves where the boards were vertical under the almost 90-degree angle that set the pitch of the roof. There was little overhang to the eaves and the gutter-less roof was corrugated metal. It looked an unfortunate arrangement, for when it rained, the water from the porch roof must sheet down onto the steps in front of the door.

The windows had no frame or trim, and no glass, but were hung with shutters, behind which curtains were loosely strung across the lower two-thirds.

Beside the house was the spiderweb of a satellite dish aimed almost directly upward. Washing hung out on lines. Flowers grew between the big, rounded, boulders that formed the bank along the shore. The chopped stumps of saplings revealed how someone must work to maintain their lake view. Immediately behind the house were mature mango trees. Electric and telegraph lines drooped between poles along the shore.

The house blended with the surroundings. What little cream-colored paint still clung to the grey wood, mimicked the color of the boulders. The rusty roof matched the paint color of the door, although the door panels were cream. The foundation frame beneath the house was painted sky blue, like the hulls of boats.

Whoever lived there kept the patch of dry grass in front of the door trimmed, planted those flowers, hung out the washing, and closed the shutters when necessary against the wind and rain. There was a shrub, clearly tended, with dark green palmate leaves, possibly a young breadfruit tree.

I envisioned waking up, to step into the morning just as the sun rose above the cauldron rim, the light catching the white plumage of egrets flying low over the lake. Samosir Island beyond would glow golden green, the early sunlight reflecting up onto it from the water.

The coast here was scalloped by a series of small bays which we cut across as the wind gathered strength. I left the others and paddled far out into the wind, to surf back to shore. Looking out I could only see a part of the lake from this corner, but from what I had already seen I could fill in the missing pieces. I could see the steep wall of the caldera to my right, dropping back behind the Uluan Peninsula, and follow its gentle curve, recalling how it would continue around the north end, and double back, to cradle the deep lake in its basin.

Samosir Island stood across the water from the Uluan Peninsula presenting its steep eastern scarp and gentle western dip. I could imagine the resurgent dome pushing up and cracking the lake floor. I could visualize how it had lifted the lake floor sediments, like dust on a partially opened trapdoor with hinges to the west. Possibly to the east of Samosir, beneath the deepest part of the lake, resides the creature of the underworld, the dragon *Naga Padoha,* subdued for now by the sword and irons of *Sideak Parujar.*

Racing waves frosted the water. I welcomed the leap and splash of my kayak as I pushed hard against the wind. Finally, I turned. My heart was in the lake and I wanted to savor the joy of paddling here, to the last possible drop. But for all my pressing upwind, the waves and the wind took just moments to sweep me to shore, to the place where we had started.

Just as when we first left, the onshore wind and waves complicated things. It was an awkward landing, first onto the jostling boat, and then up the steep crumbling bank to shore. Kids hung out like monkeys in the branches of the tree above. Passers-by stopped to watch us.

We carried the kayaks and all the gear to the hotel parking lot by the back entrance, and then, those of us who would, cracked open Bintang beers to honor the completion of our paddling journey.

We would stay here tonight at this hotel, so there was little urgency. We could sponge dry our kayaks, seal them up and wander inside to check in. Syahrul helped us carry our bags up the flights of stairs to find our room, where we could shower and change and begin cleaning our gear.

Later, we gathered beside the busy street from the hotel, across from our chosen restaurant. Although it was not a wide road, just a single lane in each direction, the traffic sped down the hill and around the bend at breakneck speed, with rarely a gap. Having experienced some of the crazy mentality of Toba driving, I did not expect responsible drivers like Syahrul or Pak Uli. We hovered and feinted in line at the side of the road. Then with a deep breath and a shout, we took off together at a run between the traffic. We knew we were back in town.

Still boisterous with adrenalin, we barged upstairs into the dimly lit bar-restaurant, filling it with chaotic bustle as we commandeered a long table. There was Saleh, his skin much sun darkened since the start. Ade wore a fluorescent green sponsor covered T-shirt, and he sipped from his ice-choked glass through the environmentally friendly stainless-steel drinking straw he always carried. Syahrul sat a little aside, slouched, gazing into his cellphone, and melting into his chair. The glow from his screen lit his serious face in the semi-darkness of the room. It was later that I learned how he only heard of his wife's pregnancy while away. It must have been hard for them to be apart.

Tandon, curly hair tousled, beard grown fuller, and tan darker, sat close to Ally. He looked content. Priyo, almost relaxing at last, with outstretched hands, lightly fingered the frosting on a tall green bottle. He smiled to himself, deep in thought. The successful outcome of all his organization was finally beginning to sink in. We ate chicken, noodles, and sambal, and drank Bintang beer.

That night, back at the hotel, we learned the difference between the expensive and less expensive rooms. One side of the hotel, with air conditioning, faced the lake. The other, with non-functioning air conditioning units, was above the busy street. We threw the window wide for some air, but the room rapidly filled with exhaust fumes from the traffic. With no mufflers on the trucks and motorcycles, traffic roared past until late in the night. The noise and fumes returned in the early morning forcing us to close the window again. Then with no reason to hurry we lazed on the giant bed, sipping coffee, and making notes in our journals, until it seemed late enough for breakfast. It was so different from the cool calm of the King's house.

31. King Sisingamangaraja XII memorial

Swina sat proudly at a table in the hotel courtyard, wearing a brightly colored jungle-print outfit, with bold patterns of parrots and big leaves. Priyo sat beside her, nibbling at breakfast from the buffet inside. This courtyard backed onto a low building that housed machines which clattered loudly with a pleasant rhythm. Kristin thought it was the sound of printing machines, but here were mechanical looms.

The rhythm was loud, reminding me of how quietly the women worked the hand looms. Theirs followed a gentle irregular process, batting the thread tight, lifting the correct threads of warp to continue the pattern, passing the shuttle through. They played the threads skillfully, fingering the warp when necessary, like a harp.

Somehow the clatter of the machines at breakfast made me think of the Industrial Revolution in England, when first water-powered, and then steam powered looms were adopted. The efficiency of the machines made it unprofitable to weave with a handloom, and weavers were left with no option but to work in the factories.

Here in Toba, fabric woven on a handloom has a higher value than machine-woven cloth. Any inconsistencies in the weave only add character. Each piece is unique, produced using hard-earned skills and labor. Each handwoven piece is something to be treasured and respected.

Kristin had intended to buy fabric at the Baligé market, but Swina, Alley and Tandon recommended a souvenir shop they thought preferable. "There you can find everything you need in one place."

Pak Uli drove us, and then sat aside with me while the shoppers deliberated. "True, there is plenty to choose from," Kristin said, coming away with several pieces, "but less variety than at the market."

Feeling as if we were beginning to know our way around, we ate again at the pork restaurant by the market before heading to visit the grave of King Sisingamangaraja XII.

"This is the grave of my clan," said Pak Uli, his hand resting gently on his heart in respect. Barefoot, we walked closer to the monument. All gloss black-tiled, two substantial cube-shapes stood, one either side, supporting a square column maybe six meters tall (twenty feet). King Sisingamangaraja XII rests in the taller column, flanked by the two of his sons who fell with him that day in 1907, Patuan Nagari and Patuan Anggi. Sadly, his beloved 17-year-old daughter, Lopian, who died in his arms that same day, could not be buried with them.

As I stood there in contemplation, my feet cried out. We could have cooked eggs on the sun-seared tiles. Deterred from lingering, we hurried back to our shoes.

Close by stood an empty museum. Decorative carving on the façade included figures galloping on horseback, and infantry on foot. This museum, dedicated in 2010, was already derelict. I suspect the building was restored to serve as a museum, just until the new museum buildings were completed nearby. If so, it enjoyed but a short lifetime as a museum. Since the door was open, we entered to find a few display-stands and tables in the entrance hall. There was a glass-doored wall cabinet with leaflets and old books and files, and a lot of dead flies. On the wall hung a painting of Sisingamangaraja XII, looking imposing, square faced and heavy jawed. Another framed portrait showed him saddled on a white horse.

Opposite and uphill of this building stood a Dutch colonial style building with glass windows. Above, and in the upper panel of the open door, were square and rectangular panes of mold-poured and patterned colored glass; green, orange, and yellow. This building too appeared to be derelict, but it was locked.

Outside stood one of the motorized rickshaws, the tuk-tuks, we saw on the roads. Built like a motorcycle and sidecar, the rectangular chassis of this sidecar was big enough to accommodate four passengers, two each side, facing each other on bench seats.

The box shape compartment was metal framed, supporting a roof that extended sideways to also shelter the motorcycle, and a plastic windshield that ran in front of both sidecar and motorcycle. Side walls with clear plastic windows left an open entrance on both sides. Outside at the back, behind the back seat, an open baggage compartment held a motorcycle helmet. Nearly every tuk-tuk was a little different in some way, customized to suit the owner.

This intriguing contraption was powered by an old single-cylinder Honda MegaPro motorcycle, probably from the early 2,000s, with its wire spoked wheels. The almost 150cc engine seemed inadequate for the purpose. I wondered how it could tackle any hill when carrying passengers.

Curious to examine it closer, I stuck my head inside, only to recoil. There was a body curled up on the back seat. I peeked again. Someone, probably the driver, was taking an afternoon siesta, fast asleep.

Tandon intended to film and record each of us reading a poem by Sitor Situmorang, but outside the hotel was too windy and loud for recording sound. We drove toward the lake shore to find a more sheltered location, dropping steeply down a narrow winding road cut into precipitous slopes, with road edges without barriers. Oncoming cars zipped into view mid-road, speeding uphill, pressing us to the edge. Kristin, never comfortable riding close to steep drops in high places, closed her eyes. We were heading for a place called Meat, and we would be meat if just one of these reckless uphill speeders miscalculated.

The small ferry landing at Meat might have served us well, had another group with a similar idea not got there first. Three girls posed in short, sexy, matching navy-blue outfits, with long diaphanous shawls that drifted out in the breeze. While they sang or mimed to pop songs blasted from an impressive sound system, cameramen crept around them recording video. An impromptu audience stood looking on.

The loud music precluded our own recording, so there was little to do but enjoy the moment and watch the action. A little offshore, a man fished from his solu, beneath the steep green mountainside, no doubt listening to the music in the way we so often had from the water.

Hoping to find a quieter spot on the clifftop at the edge of the caldera, we jumped back into the cars to climb the hill, revisiting Kristin's harrowing nemesis again on the ascent. We would return to the same viewpoint we visited at the start of our trip.

The vista from there, looking out across the lake toward Samosir Island, was stunning. I watched the pattern of swells refract around the headland way down below us, bending to meet the curve of the beach in the bay. Rebounding waves from the cliff crisscrossed back out in a slow dance.

Around us on the summit, studding the grass, stood the tall multilayered mausoleums, some with the traditional house shape at the uppermost layer. Here was a hilltop village for the dead, but it did not feel like a graveyard. Somehow, I think of graveyards as being places where the dead hide away together, places that are visited from time to time by the living, with the sole purpose of remembering the dead. Here on the other hand, sarcophagi are scattered around where people gather to view the lake, where motorcycle food carts trundle up to sell sate padang, and bakso. Lovers meet here. Adolescents kick back with kreteks and tuak. The dead and the living rejoice together.

Tandon posed us each in turn near the cliff edge. There, with the lake behind, we read out loud our choice of one of Sitor Situmorang's poems in Bahasa Indonesia, or in English translation. Tandon then shot our portraits with the same backdrop.

Returning to Piltik, we received a warm welcome from the barista. Instantly recalling my last coffee order of a latte and an Americano, she offered to make me the same again while we checked into our room. Now we said our goodbyes to Pak Uli, Syahrul having already quietly slipped away, anxious to be home with his wife.

When Tigor and Vera arrived, Tigor presented me with amazing, printed, photo portraits chosen from those he took in the studio before our trip. His son, Tim, flew out specially with them today from Jakarta. I felt honored.

Vera's treat for us tonight was an amazing meal of spicy chicken, eggplant, beans, carrots, squash, and afterward pineapple pudding with a latte. There, dining at the restaurant also was a band of musicians with their sound engineers, and a motorcycle group on tour staying overnight. Vera stood and clapped for attention. She confidently introduced each group, explaining where they were from, and what they had been doing. Everyone, she said, must be less reserved and have a starting point for mingling between the groups. We would see the motorcyclists again in the morning before they left, and meet the band on our way to Jakarta, but in the meantime, Vera served tuak to lubricate our last evening.

32. A Time to Reflect

We awoke to a slow, grinding, blues tune. The Rolling Stones were singing, *You've Got to Move*: the alarm on my phone. I made coffee in our room using hot water from a flask, left for us on the table outside, and sachets of instant coffee remaining from our previous trip in West Papua. A pitiful substitute for Piltik coffee, but just what I needed to wake me before I crossed to the covered courtyard, just a few paces away, to order lattes. There we relaxed for a few minutes in the increasing light of dawn until Tandon and Ally joined us, at just before seven.

The four of us planned to record some interviews in the quiet of the early morning. We quickly set everything up ready, on the lower hidden deck, in front of the scarecrows adjacent to the rice fields.

The cool mist over the lowest ground rapidly dissolved. Water chuckled down the concrete culvert beside us and birds zipped past and chirped from the bushes. One by one, from the top, the low morning sun caught the horizontal shallow-stepped terraces. Layer by layer, each terrace fired from lackluster to rich glowing golden green. The rice stood stiff as stubble, bathed from the side by the first of the morning's warmth.

Kristin and I sipped our coffee as Tandon adjusted our hidden microphones and tested for sound. Then he and Ally each filmed from a different angle as first I, then Kristin, talked about different aspects of our trip. Priyo had listed some questions.

"What did you discover about the paddle culture on Lake Toba? What is it like to paddle a solu? How does it feel to stay in Batak houses? How do you interact with Batak people?"

The sun grew hotter by the minute, the light more intense. This close to the equator, the moments of special morning light around dawn are precious, but fleeting. The light hardens rapidly.

Our interviews drifted into the realm of poets and poetry, and Batak values. In his poem, *Island on an Island,* Sitor Situmorang set the scene: *Six continents, the seven seas I've traveled...* before pondering which place was the most beautiful. For many that would be an impossible question to answer, but not for Sitor. Beside Lake Toba was where his journey, and his life began. Beside Lake Toba is where he wanted his bones to rest. He had traveled, sometimes stopping for a short time here or there, occasionally making a new home, once as a prisoner. He stayed in many places during changing times. His final return says a lot about loyalty, Toba Batak sentiment and culture.

Yet, Sitor observes in his poem, *Baligé,* looking back at that town he first knew some fifty years before, that *Nothing seems to have changed in this small town...* But he realizes how both he and Baligé must have changed. He had come back, but it was not the same. A common realization that he expresses well.

Time and space are embodied in the Batak ulos. I cannot read an ulos, cannot distinguish one that is good in the traditional sense from one that is less so. I can only favor according to my own aesthetics. Yet the ulos is complicated. By process, one end must be older than the other. It takes time to complete an ulos on the loom. The clock ticks as the yarn sets out on its journey, starts to porpoise over and under the warps. Along with her skill, the weaver's time is captured, not as a snapshot, but as if in a journal. Batak textiles represent a value beyond their usefulness as garments and their beauty.

Our journey, *The Heart of Toba*, offered me a glimpse into another culture. It opened a window for me to see a new place from my own perspective. I found myself in the warm embrace of the Toba Batak ulos. I could see why people are called to return. Now, from here, I realized I should take a moment to compare, to look back with critical eyes at my own culture.

Our interviews complete, we waited for breakfast, at ease. That was where Tigor and Vera found us. They must leave shortly, so we would have all too little time to talk. Yet even then, to interrupt us, came thunder as first one, and then another hefty-sounding machine burst into life. There on the gravel drive stood the gang of gleaming Harley-Davidson motorcycles, chrome gleaming, paintwork immaculate, sturdy paniers loaded for the journey. They grumbled, and growled, clearing their throats while the group we met last night said their goodbyes and donned helmets. The riders were finally ready to mount and leave.

The rumbling and shaking rose to a roaring crescendo as they eased from the drive. With tyres scrunching, they turned onto the road. One after the other they accelerated away.

As the clamor faded, I stood deep in thought, staring into space. Suddenly focusing on the shrubs that I was inadvertently staring at by the dining area, I realized they were coffee bushes. Everything Vera Hutauruk and Tigor Siahaan planted here was for a reason.

Epilogue

Priyo would accompany us to the airport, to make sure everything went smoothly. He smiled when Ade joked that he was making certain we really left, but he was coming as a kindness in case of some hitch; should we need help. Now, with both Pak Uli and Syahrul gone, we had a new driver. This ride was to leave a parting reminder of the fatalistic driving so prevalent here.

From the back seat, I watched the road ahead twist and turn, as we flew past small motorcycles with two or three people clinging on board. A boy who looked about ten years old, came at us on a motorcycle far too big for him. As he raced toward us, he swooped confidently around a pothole in the middle of the road, and then with a joyful smile at us, swerved away at the last minute to narrowly miss us.

We finally slowed behind a truck carrying pineapples. Our driver hovered along the center of the road, pulling aside barely enough for a tuk-tuk to pass us, side view mirrors almost shaving.

Then he felt he had waited too long. It was a winding road but driving slowly was not his style. He put his foot down to accelerate along the side of the pineapple truck. I watched the blind bend ahead as we ran side by side along the narrow road. Then a truck sped into view. It flashed its lights repeatedly. Surely our driver would drop back to safety, but no. With the gap closing fast, he jammed his hand on the horn, as if that would help us go faster. We blasted onward toward almost certain doom. There was nowhere for the oncoming truck to go.

We just made it past the pineapple truck, squeezing in by a whisker as the two trucks scissored together and shot past in a moment. We had darted aside so late; I could guess at the oncoming driver's fury. I felt the pineapple truck driver's curses hot against the back of my neck, and I took a breath.

Our driver was grinning. We were hovering once more, ready to gamble as we approached the next bend, passing, pausing, hovering. I crossed my fingers. I felt the car accelerate again, heard the horn blare.

Ade was booked on the same flight as us, and at the baggage check was there to translate, explaining that our bags were overweight. We would have to pay 600,000 rupiah, about $40 US in cash. Neither credit cards nor debit cards were acceptable. We must find cash.

Ade waited with me and the baggage, caring for us till the end, while Kristin hurried from the terminal to find an ATM. Finally, she rejoined the line toward the security check. It was very last minute when we hurried across the asphalt to the plane and climbed the metal steps. Sitting together in a row, we all three slept for the duration of the flight to Jakarta.

Flying onward from Jakarta, quite a few passengers wore face masks. But at Taipei airport, and then on the flight from Taiwan to Seattle, all the air crew and most of the passengers wore masks. It seemed bizarre.

Unbeknown to us, while we were away and insulated from the news, Coronavirus Covid19 had made its appearance. Not yet a pandemic, it was about to close the door on our Lake Toba trip. Life was about to change for many people, including us. Seattle would become the first epicenter of the infection in USA. Less than two weeks after we returned home, Seattle began to lock down and encourage self-isolation.

Little did I know that I was about to spend my summer at home, for the first time since moving here. Or how this would give me time to reflect on Lake Toba, and the wonderful people we met there. Instead of embarking on my usual travel schedule, I would explore what sparked my curiosity about Lake Toba. I found it a luxury to have so much undivided time to apply to researching and writing. It gave me time to embark on a different kind of journey.

Acknowledgments

Experiencing and writing about Toba has been like creating a painting, not alone, but with the gentle brushstrokes of many people. From the start I must thank Nicklas Millegård for introducing me to Indonesia, and Priyo Utomo and Swina Montororing, whose vision brought me to Lake Toba. Thanks to the rest of the wonderful on-water team, Ade Satari, Saleh Alatas, Tandon: Don Seco, Allysa Shim, Harriet Huber, and Kristin Nelson, also Evendi Piliang, and Roosen Manurung. On land, thank you Syahrul Alamsyah, and Pak Uli Lumbangaol.

My particular thanks to Saut Hutauruk, Vera Hutauruk, Edward Tigor Siahaan, and Iman Situmorang, all pivotal to making this project happen.

Expedition sponsors include National Geographic Indonesia, Piltik Homestay and Piltik Coffee, Point 65 Sweden, Eiger, T. Kardin Pisau Indonesia and Rudy Project.

Many people of Toba opened their hearts and homes to us throughout our trip, making our experience incredibly special. Just a few of you appear in this book, but this heartfelt thank you is to all of you. If I left a little of me at Toba, and if Toba has become a part of me, this is largely because of you.

Thanks to the Sitor Situmorang Foundation, and The Lontar Foundation, Jakarta, for me permitting me to include poetry by Sitor Situmorang.

Acknowledgements

In fact-checking and proof-reading, I very much valued the help of Elizabeth Foster, Michael Muller, Richard Öhman, Priyo Utomo, Ade Satari, and Iman Situmorang.

Finally, and by no means least, thank you Kristin Nelson. Not only were you a wonderful companion on Lake Toba, but your help throughout the writing of this book, in proof reading and offering tips and suggestions were especially valuable. It would not have been the same story without you!

Bibliography

Bonatz, Dominik. Miksic, John. Neidel, J. David. Tjoa-Bonatz, Mai Lin. *From Distant Tales: Archaeology and Ethnohistory in the Highlands of Sumatra.* Cambridge Scholars Pub. 2009.

Bowles, Philip, *Rediscovery of Modigliani's nose-horned lizard, Harpesaurus modiglianii vinciguerra, 1933 (reptilia: agamidae) after 129 years without any observation.* major article: 03 TAPROBANICA VOL. 09: NO. 01 urn: lsid:zoobank.org:pub:9A280171-C87D-4718-BFA7-139E21FEE2CC. 2020.

Burgess, Anthony *(1993) [1956]. The Long Day Wanes: A Malayan Trilogy. W. W. Norton & Company 1993.*

Chesner, C. A. *The Toba Complex*, Quaternary International (2011) doi:10.1016/j.quaint.2011.09.025 (PDF).

Coetzee, J. Jones, R. & Hill, M. (2014). Biodiversity and Conservation, 23(5), *Water hyacinth, Eichhornia crassipes (Pontederiaceae), reduces benthic macroinvertebrate diversity in a protected subtropical lake in South Africa.* 1319-1330.

Doubrawa, Irene. Lehner, Erich. Rieger-Jandl, Andrea. (eds.) *Village Architecture in Sumatra: A comparative study: Toba Batak, Karo Batak, Minangkabau.* IVA-ICRA, Vienna, Austria 2016.

Drori, Jonathan. *Around the World in 80 Trees.* Laurence King Publishing 2018.

Elio Modigliani, Tusca National Museum of Anthropology and Ethnology Section of the Natural History Museum Exhibition Guide 2002.

Ginting, N. Rahman, N. Vinky. and. Sembiring, G. *Tourism Development Based on Geopark in Bakkara Caldera Toba*

Bibliography

Indonesia. 2016. IOP Conf. Series Materials science and engineering 180 (2017) 012086. doi: 10, 1088/1757-899X/180/1/012086 (PDF).

Ikegami, Shigehiro. *Historical Changes of Toba Batak Reburial Tombs: A Case Study of a Rural Community in the Central Highland of North Sumatra.* Southeast Asian Studies, Vol. 34, No.4, March 1997.

Lambanraja, Victor. *Tourism Area Life Cycle in Lake Toba.* PDF ISSN 0024-9521. IJG Vol. 44 #2 December 2012 (150-160)

MacLean, Alistair. *Captain Cook.* Doubleday and Co. Inc 1972

Marsden, William. *The History of Sumatra.* J. H. Creery 1811.

Multatuli. *Max Havelaar, Or, the Coffee Auctions of the Dutch Trading Company.* New York Review Book, translation 2019.

Norden, Hermann. *From Golden Gate to Golden Sun: A record of travel, sport and observation in Siam and Malaya.* Boston, Small Maynard & Company Publishers 1923.

Niessen, S. A. *Legacy in Cloth: Batak Textiles of Indonesia,* Leiden, KITLV Press 2009.

Niessen, S.A. *Motifs of Life in Toba Batak Texts and Textiles.* Foris Publications 1985.

Nurdiah, Esti Asih *Protruding Saddle Roof Structure of Toraja, Minang and Toba Batak House: Learning from Traditional Structure System* Department of Architecture, Faculty of Civil Engineering and Planning, Petra Christian University, Indonesia, (2011) (PDF).

Purba, Mauly. *Review of research into the Gondang Sabangunan musical genre in Batak Toba Society of North Sumatra.* Etnomusikologi Vol. 1 #1 Mei (2005) 38-64.

Rev. Thompson, W. M. *Memoirs of the Rev. Samuel Munson, and the Rev. Henry Lyman, late missionaries to the Indian Archipelago, with the journal of their exploring tour.* Appleton 1843.

Bibliography

Sibeth, Achim. *The Batak. Peoples of the Island of Sumatra.* Thames and Hudson 1991.

Situmorang, Sitor. *To Love, To Wander: the poetry of Sitor Situmorang*, The Lontar Foundation, Jakarta 1996.

Situmorang, Sitor. *Oceans of Longing.* Silkworm Books 2018.

Situmorang, Sitor. *Red Gerberas.* Silkworm Books 2018.

Snoek, Kees. *Obituary, Sitor Situmorang.* Wacana Volume 16 #1 (2015) 243-248.

Susila, Wayan R. *Targeted Study of the Arabica Coffee Production Chain in North Sumatra* (The Mandheling Coffee) Jakarta 2005 Annex-E.5. (PDF).

Tanakamaru, Haruya. Kato, Tomoyuki. Takara Kaoru. *Water Levels Lake Toba Electricity. Water Balance Analysis and Water Level Simulation of Lake Toba Indonesia.* 56-OHS-A606. (PDF).

Teanglum, A. Teanglum, S. Saithong, *A. Selection of Indigo Plant Varieties and Other Plants that Yield Indigo Dye.* I-SEEC2011. (2011).

Wallace, A. Russel. *On the Bamboo and Durian of Borneo, (In a letter to Sir W.T. Hooker.)* 1856. Included in Volume 8 of Hookers's Journal of Botany.

Winokur, Jon, *The Traveling Curmudgeon: Irreverent Notes, Quotes, and Anecdotes on Dismal Destinations, Excess Baggage, the Full Upright Position, and Other Reasons Not to Go There.* Sasquatch Books Seattle, 2003.

Improving-the-Water-Quality-of-Lake-Toba-Indonesia. (PDF). World Bank Group Report # AUS0000463.

Population of Indonesia by village, (PDF) result of 2010 population census.

The Geographic Journal (PDF) Royal Geographical Society, Great Britain, 1896, (Re: Length of solus).